D0480687

The Shakespeare Handbooks

THE SHAKESPEARE HANDBOOKS

Series Editor: John Russell Brown

PUBLISHED

FORTHCOMING

The Shakespeare Handbooks

Antony and Cleopatra

Bridget Escolme

palgrave
macmillan

© Bridget Escolme 2006

All rights reserved. No reproduction, copy or transmission of this publication may be made without written permission.

No paragraph of this publication may be reproduced, copied or transmitted save with written permission or in accordance with the provisions of the Copyright, Designs and Patents Act 1988, or under the terms of any licence permitting limited copying issued by the Copyright Licensing Agency, 90 Tottenham Court Road, London W1T 4LP.

Any person who does any unauthorised act in relation to this publication may be liable to criminal prosecution and civil claims for damages.

The author has asserted her right to be identified as the author of this work in accordance with the Copyright, Designs and Patents Act 1988.

First published 2006 by
PALGRAVE MACMILLAN
Houndmills, Basingstoke, Hampshire RG21 6XS and
175 Fifth Avenue, New York, N.Y. 10010
Companies and representatives throughout the world

PALGRAVE MACMILLAN is the global academic imprint of the Palgrave Macmillan division of St. Martin's Press, LLC and of Palgrave Macmillan Ltd. Macmillan® is a registered trademark in the United States, United Kingdom and other countries. Palgrave is a registered trademark in the European Union and other countries.

ISBN 978-1-4039-4206-7 hardback

ISBN 978-1-4039-4207-4   ISBN 978-0-230-80423-4 (eBook)
DOI 10.1007/978-0-230-80423-4

A catalogue record for this book is available from the British Library.

A catalog record for this book is available from the Library of Congress

10	9	8	7	6	5	4	3	2	1
15	14	13	12	11	10	09	08	07	06

For my brother, John

Contents

General Editor's Preface

The Shakespeare Handbooks provide an innovative way of studying the theatrical life of the plays. The commentaries, which are their core feature, enable a reader to envisage the words of a text unfurling in performance, involving actions and meanings not readily perceived except in rehearsal or performance. The aim is to present the plays in the environment for which they were written and to offer an experience as close as possible to an audience's progressive experience of a production.

While each book has the same range of contents, their authors have been encouraged to shape them according to their own critical and scholarly understanding and their first-hand experience of theatre practice. The various chapters are designed to complement the commentaries: the cultural context of each play is presented together with quotations from original sources; the authority of its text or texts is considered with what is known of the earliest performances; key performances and productions of its subsequent stage history are both described and compared. The aim in all this has been to help readers to develop their own informed and imaginative view of a play in ways that supplement the provision of standard editions and are more user-friendly than detailed stage histories or collections of criticism from diverse sources.

Further volumes are in preparation so that, within a few years, the Shakespeare Handbooks will be available for all the plays that are frequently studied and performed.

John Russell Brown

Acknowledgements

First, and most importantly, I would like to thank John Russell Brown, general editor of the *Shakespeare Handbooks*, for his kindness, patience and invaluable suggestions. Sonya Barker and Kate Wallis at Palgrave Macmillan have been wonderfully friendly, efficient and tolerant throughout the publication process. Staff at the Workshop Theatre and the School of English at the University of Leeds, particularly Frances Babbage, Martin Butler and David Lindley, have given generous encouragement, support, suggestions and, in David's case, previews of forthcoming work. Students at the Workshop Theatre made contributions, often unwittingly, through their generous participation in practical classes, and Masters graduate Sarah Lann deserves singling out for the inspiration provided by her own work on Cleopatra and beauty. Many thanks to the archivists at the Globe and the Shakespeare Birthplace Trust and to David Bevington for generous responses to queries. Thanks as always to my parents Bob and Hilary Escolme and my brother John for their support, and to Rich Barlow for unfailing encouragement and permission to create chaos in his work space yet again.

1 *The Text and Early Performances*

Note how simply the producer overcomes the old problem . . . of lifting the body of Antony 10 or 12 feet high into the monument. No struggling with ropes; no scene change here to ruin a good speech or a smooth performance.

(Review of *Antony and Cleopatra, Evesham Journal*, 5 May 1945)

CLEOPATRA   Here's sport indeed! How heavy weighs my lord!
    Our strength is all gone into heaviness,
    That makes this weight. Had I great Juno's power,
    The strong-winged Mercury should fetch thee up
    And set thee by Jove's side. Yet come a little;
    Wishers were ever fools. O, come, come, come!
        They heave Antony aloft to Cleopatra.

(IV.xvi.33–8)

The reviewer above is delighted at the simplicity of Robert Atkins's 1945 production of *Antony and Cleopatra*. Here, he is relieved to note, are none of the extravagant scene changes that, during the previous century, had broken the smooth transition from one fictional location to another that the play suggests. But this is not the only thing that pleases. The reviewer is also happy not to be distracted by any 'struggling with ropes'. A struggle, however, is something that the text itself appears to require. As Cleopatra remarks herself, a smooth transition from ground to monument, one that would permit the smooth delivery of a good speech, would be possible were she a goddess. But the queen and her attendants – and the young men that would have played them in Shakespeare's theatre – are only foolish, wishing humans; to dispense with the struggle with ropes here would seem to necessitate dispensing with the speech.

If the reviewer expected this scene to offer an emotional through-line, unbroken by any awkward physical struggle, this book is going to argue that he was missing something about this play's daring shifts from tragedy to comedy, from mythic grandeur to material reality, from fictional to theatrical world. The theatre buildings and the audience for which Shakespeare wrote *Antony and Cleopatra* are partly responsible for the kind of play it is, and the meanings it produces in performance. This does not mean that historical reconstruction is the best way of staging the play. It does mean that it is worth considering the different versions of the play that are produced by the theatrical rules and assumptions of Shakespeare's time and of later periods. In Atkins's case they seem to be rules of tragic decorum and assumptions about the 'smoothness' provided by Shakespeare's open stage. In this *Shakespeare Handbook*, I begin with a discussion of the theatres for which Shakespeare wrote, and in which the play might have been performed. I want to argue that an awareness of the kinds of performances Elizabethan and Jacobean theatres produced will usefully allow Shakespeare to be strange as well as familiar, historically alien as well as recognisable and relevant.

Antony and Cleopatra in the Jacobean theatre

By the end of Shakespeare's career, the King's Men – the company for which he wrote his plays and in which he was an actor and shareholder – not only owned the open-air public playhouse the Globe, but had sole use of a private, indoor theatre, the Blackfriars. It is not known in which of these theatres *Antony and Cleopatra* was first performed, as there is no record of a performance of the play until over a century after Shakespeare's death. The play has an entry in the Lord Chamberlain's records of 1669, which states that it was 'formerly acted at the Blackfriars'. It may well have been, but this does not mean it was first acted there. It was first entered in the Stationer's Register, the record of publishing rights, in 1608, and plays often had their first performances around the time that they were registered. Though they took a lease at the Blackfriars in 1608, the King's Men are not likely to have had their first full season there until 1610. A majority of scholars are now convinced that Shakespeare wrote *Antony and Cleopatra* during the second half of 1606 or at the beginning of 1607. If this is so, Shakespeare will have had the Globe in mind when writing the play, even if it was later performed at the Blackfriars. Wherever the first performance took place, however, it is significant that Shakespeare was writing for actors who were used to being surrounded, on almost all sides, by audience members they could see. At the Globe, with its day-lit thrust stage, this is obvious. But even in the Blackfriars, where more in the way of lighting effects could be produced, candles in the auditorium would not have been put out during the performance, and seats were to be had not only in galleries adjacent to the stage, but on the stage itself. In this account of *Antony and Cleopatra*, then, attention is paid to characters' relationships with the audience as well as relationships between characters.

The architecture of Elizabethan and Jacobean theatres suggests a much more fluid relationship between stage and auditorium than the proscenium arch theatres of the Victorian and Edwardian periods, in which Shakespeare is still sometimes performed today. Indeed, lighting designers and performers still sometimes create a fictional world for the play as if it existed separately from the theatre in which the production takes place, even where modern theatre architecture offers the potential for a more direct relationship between performer and audience. I have argued elsewhere that early modern plays are peopled by figures who have both fictional and theatrical intentions or objectives (see *Talking to the Audience*, 2005). This is particularly important in a play that is so much concerned with display and reputation. Antony and Cleopatra have a paying as well as a court audience to play to. These characters know they are being watched.

The Globe

The Globe was built near the south bank of the river Thames in 1599, by the theatrical entrepreneur James Burbage, for Shakespeare's company, then called the Chamberlain's Men. The theatre was a circular building, with a canopied stage thrusting out into a yard and surrounded by three tiers of seating galleries. The 'groundlings' paid a penny to stand in the yard; a seat cost two or three pence. A façade, known as the *frons scaenae*, was positioned at what we might now think of as the back of the stage. The galleries set into the *frons* contained not only a balcony in which scenes could take place, but private boxes in which a seat cost a shilling. The position of these expensive Lords' Rooms suggests that our notions of up and down stage did not pertain to Shakespeare's theatre – the players must have addressed the Lords' Rooms as well as lower-paying playgoers – and that being seen as well as seeing was an important motivation for attending the theatre. Below the galleries, the *frons* had two doors for entrances and exits, either side of a central recess through which larger props – a throne or a bed for Cleopatra's death, for example – could be brought on stage. Characters could be revealed in this central 'discovery space', though it is unlikely that whole scenes would have been played there, as was once thought.

Open and uncluttered with scenery, the Globe provided Shakespeare's players with an appropriately fluid space for a play like *Antony and Cleopatra*, with its frequent changes in location. The play repeatedly sets up opposing sides, by having potential rivals enter in conversation from each door, and by marching opposing armies across the stage. The large, open stage space and its entrances facilitate all this. The sense of events happening over huge expanses of the known world, and the expansiveness of some of the language in the play, has been enough to suggest to some scholars that this is a play more suited to the Globe than to the Blackfriars.

The challenge of hauling the dying Antony into Cleopatra's monument has been met in a variety of ways in modern production, and no final scholarly conclusions have been reached as to how the King's Men would have managed it. If it is assumed that Antony is hauled aloft to the gallery at the Globe, there is the problem of visibility to be accounted for. The gallery may have been fronted by a balustrade (which would have meant some extra hauling to lift Antony over it), and, even if the smallest of the speculated measurements for the Globe theatre are correct, what happened there would not have dominated the stage space visually, as one might expect the protagonist's last agonies to do, even in a period when playgoers spoke of going to 'hear' rather than 'see' a play. If Cleopatra is holding Antony in her arms on the floor of the gallery, he might be hardly seen from behind the balustrade at all. Andrew Gurr solves the problem by arguing that a number of plays prove that 'there must in fact have been . . . a raised platform, or even a curtained booth set up on stage, of the kind used in the early years by the traveling players as their tiring house'. This could have been used as 'a "monument" big enough to hold Antony's body and several women on top, but low enough for the women to lift the body up onto it' (Gurr, *The Shakespearean Stage*, p. 149). Others have argued that the wounded Antony could have been brought on stage in a chair, which was then attached to a pulley and winched to the Gallery by Cleopatra and her attendants. Whatever the solution, Cleopatra's speech above indicates the effort needed to haul Antony in this scene.

Though the platform stage of both the indoor and the outdoor playhouses offered nothing in the way of extravagant or naturalistic scenic effects, visual spectacle was to be had by way of costumes. Costumes for the leads were often costly, sometimes handed down from the aristocratic patrons of the companies. Evidence from the only surviving artistic representation of a play of the time – Henry Peacham's drawing of a scene from *Titus Andronicus* – shows the smaller roles wearing contemporary dress, whilst the leading actors wear approximations of classical dress, including a short toga and a laurel wreath for Titus. Roman costume might, then, have been provided for the triumvirate and their close associates in *Antony and Cleopatra*. Cleopatra's call for Charmian to 'cut [her] lace' at I.iii.71 suggests a Jacobean bodice for Cleopatra, though there might have been something more Eastern to enhance it, particularly when she calls for her robes in Act V.

With regard to music, *Antony and Cleopatra* is a noisy play, with trumpet flourishes to accompany many of the formal entries in the play, and drums and trumpets to open battle scenes. Until the turn of the sixteenth century, it is likely that this music would have come from the tiring house behind the *frons*, rather than from a specially designated music room above the Globe stage. Gurr suggests that this would have changed around 1607–9, near the time when *Antony and Cleopatra* was written, and the King's Men acquired their permanent indoor home, the Blackfriars. At around this time, playwrights producing plays for the outdoor playhouses started dividing their plays into Acts, suggesting more complex inter-Act music played on string and woodwind instruments, like that to be heard at the indoor playhouses. This music would have been better heard from one of the Lords' Rooms taken over for the purpose. The First Folio (F1) stage direction makes clear that the 'hautboys', or oboes, which create the mysterious atmosphere of Act IV, scene iii, are played beneath the stage. This may well have been more resonant and effective at the indoor playhouse.

The Blackfriars

James Burbage bought and converted rooms in the old Blackfriars' monastery in 1596 for the Chamberlain's Men, but local residents stopped him from using it for such a purpose by petition to the Privy Council, on the grounds that a theatre in their area would be a noisy and immoral nuisance. After his death in 1597, Burbage's sons leased the Blackfriars playhouse to a children's company, the Children of the Chapel, and Keith Sturgess notes that this new occupancy was clearly not considered such a threat to local law and order (Sturgess, *Jacobean Private Theatre*, p. 2). In 1603, patronage of Shakespeare's company was taken over by James I, and they became the King's Men; there was no repeat banning order when the manager of the Children of the Chapel leased the Blackfriars back to the adult players in 1608. After two years in which a plague epidemic made performances unlikely, the King's Men had a permanent indoor home, and would spend the winter playing the Blackfriars and the summer at the Globe, until the closing of the theatres in 1643.

The playing space at the Blackfriars probably shared some features of the outdoor playhouse. The very fact that the King's Men evidently had little trouble performing the same repertory in each space would suggest similarities. Like the Globe, the Blackfriars was likely to have had galleries of seats, a central tiring-house opening with an exit either side, a playing space on an upper level above the opening, and a platform stage, albeit a platform walled in by private boxes rather than thrusting out into a yard. Physically as well as socially, however, playgoing there must have been quite a different experience from that offered by the Globe.

Though Emrys Jones was convinced that Shakespeare might well have at least had the Blackfriars in mind when he wrote *Antony and Cleopatra* (Jones, *Scenic Form in Shakespeare*, 1971, pp. 23–9), one of the most substantial works on the Jacobean indoor playhouse, Keith Sturgess's *Jacobean Private Theatre* does not mention it at all. Sturgess's account of the Blackfriars emphasises the intimacy of the space. The Blackfriars stage was about half the size of the Globe's and it held an audience of around one-third the size, some of whom would have paid to enter through the tiring house and sit on the stage itself, cramping the playing space still further. Having imagined *Antony and Cleopatra* on a large stage, open to the air, it is perhaps difficult to envisage armies marching across a platform half the size, cramped still further by gallants sitting on stools, and watched by an entirely seated audience (the indoor playhouse pits were full of seated playgoers, not standing groundlings).

Sturgess has noted that in plays likely to have been performed primarily or exclusively at indoor playhouses, scenes with large numbers of supernumeraries tend to be structured and ritualistic – dances or masks that involve a careful, controlled use of limited stage space. Martin White's experiments in a reconstruction of a Jacobean indoor playhouse at the University of Bristol give the impression of an almost voyeuristic relationship between performer and audience, as the latter watch the intimate grotesqueries of mannerist tragi-comedies by candlelight. It would be wrong to discount the idea of a performance of *Antony and Cleopatra* there because of its armies and worldwide settings, or the central characters' consciousness of themselves as epic figures. Modern studio productions have, after all, successfully conveyed the play's sense of the fate of the world depending on the fluctuations of a middle-aged love affair, and the candlelit intimacy of the Blackfriars could have produced an almost transgressive sense of being let into the private worlds of mythic figures. It is also worth noting that there are no on-stage battle scenes in *Antony and Cleopatra*. Action by both sea and land takes place off stage, and if a storm at sea for *The Tempest* can be produced by 'squibs from the upper level of the Blackfriars façade', 'drums in the tiring house' and a 'sea machine (small pebbles revolved in a drum)' (Sturgess, p. 81), there is no reason why a sea-fight soundscape cannot be created there too, though all these effects would have had to be created more quietly indoors than at the Globe.

More interesting when considering the play's possible tone and meaning is the combination of the intimacy of the indoor playhouse and the intellectual expectations of its audience. It would be anachronistic to argue that the smaller space produced a 'naturalistic' acting style. With audience members seated in boxes close to the stage and on the stage itself, I would argue that the notion of an actor's circle of attention limited to the world of the fiction is a counter-intuitive one. However, the limited stage space and less challenging acoustic of the indoor playhouse meant that there, actors must have stood at a distance from one another more like that in real social life than when creating imposing stage pictures to fill the Globe; broad, demonstrative gestures would have been both unnecessary and inconvenient.

What is the effect, then, of the expansive language of *Antony and Cleopatra*, the tendency of the central figures to self-dramatisation and the emphasis of their glorious position on the world stage and in the afterlife, when played in an intimate indoor space? It would perhaps have emphasised the play's ironies. As many critics have pointed out, 'noble Antony' does very little that is noble or heroic in this play. His mythic status is ironised both by Cleopatra and by his own laborious death. Lines that mythologise Antony's status and his action are potentially faintly absurd in an intimate space where the audience sits close to his demise. Cleopatra's dreamed myth of Antony (V.ii.75–99), spoken in the flickering candlelight, might seem more convincingly heroic here than Antony himself. Moreover, a Blackfriars audience, connoisseurs of mannerist pessimism and the arch, ironic commentary on the adult world provided by the Children's companies (see Sturgess, p. 6), would very likely have enjoyed the commentary on the gap between myth and reality the play potentially provides.

Imagining *Antony and Cleopatra* at the Blackfriars sheds a new social light on the celebrated meta-theatrical reference to the 'squeaking Cleopatra' that the queen dreads will 'boy [her] greatness'

(V.ii.219–20) as she is paraded through Rome by the triumphant Caesar. This is often pointed to as a daring foregrounding of the young man who plays Cleopatra in the play itself: Shakespeare must have been very confident that his company's own boy would be sure not to embarrass them with unconvincing squeaking at this point. If one accepts the argument that a young man would have played the female leads in the adult companies, rather than boys as young as those who worked for the Children's troupes, this could be seen as a dig at the Children's companies, like that to be found in *Hamlet* F1: the King's Men are too wise and professional to trust their Cleopatra to a little boy. If the play was envisaged as a Blackfriars piece, however, it was to play to the elite audiences who would have enjoyed these boys' performances, and though Shakespeare is never reluctant to poke direct and conspiratorial fun at his audience, there might also be a more flattering reference to elitist taste contained in these lines. What Cleopatra dreads most after Antony's death is being humiliated before the Roman mob, with their poor taste in food and performance, whose boy players are likely to be crude amateurs rather than the convincing professional boys the Blackfriars audience are likely to have seen at the theatre.

The players

Whether *Antony and Cleopatra* was played at the Globe, the Blackfriars or both, it is worth considering what is known about the company that played at both theatres. The King's Men were the most popular and highly regarded in late Elizabethan and Jacobean London and their actors often stayed with them for their whole working lives. The company comprised around twelve share-holding adult actors and about four boys at any one time; smaller adult roles would have been played by temporarily hired men. The boys were apprentices in the acting trade, and some would have graduated to adult roles and become shareholders themselves. How old the boy who played the challenging role of Cleopatra would have been is disputed, and students turning to the introductions of modern editions for answers will be given a range of arguments.

John Wilders' Arden edition insists that to be 'sceptical about an adolescent boy's ability to do justice to the role' is to 'underestimate the intelligence of children of that age'. He rather fudges what he takes 'that age' to be by referring to both 'boys' and 'adolescents' in his account (p. 11), but given that he compares the sophistication of the boy player with the musical ability of the modern British choir-school pupil, he is presumably thinking of boys no older than thirteen. Richard Madelaine's edition, on the other hand, tends to support the argument that boys would have continued to play women's parts into early manhood (p. 24). Not all teenage boys go through a sudden and dramatic breaking of the voice – Cordelia's was, after all 'soft, gentle and low'.

Antony would no doubt have been played by Richard Burbage; he played the leading roles in Chamberlain's/King's Men's productions from 1594 until his death in 1619. There are very few contemporary accounts available of what Burbage's or any Elizabethan and Jacobean acting would have been like, though several of the references to performance that have survived refer to Burbage. I have assumed, with others and as a result of students' practical experiments, that the outdoor playhouse demanded a more openly demonstrative style than the indoor, and Hamlet's advice to the players suggests that an over-emphatic, gestural style had become outdated by the turn of the century. A much-quoted description of Burbage by eyewitness Richard Flecknoe describes the actor as 'so wholly transforming himself into his part, and putting off himself with his clothes, as he never (not so much as in the tiring house) assum'd himself until the play was done' (in Chambers, *Elizabethan Stage*, vol. 4, p. 370). This might suggest an immersion in character not unlike that demanded by Stanislavski. There are crucial differences, though, in the relationship between performer and audience demanded by Jacobean playhouses and that produced by the proscenium arch theatres for which Stanislavski trained actors, and differences too in the ways in which psychology would have been understood by performers then and now. Throughout this *Handbook*'s account of the text, I have extended the actor's 'circle of attention', conceived by Stanislavski to prevent the performer from being distracted by the audience, to include that audience.

The First Folio text and modern editions

The line references in this *Handbook* correspond to those of the New Cambridge Shakespeare edition, edited by David Bevington; Richard Madelaine's text in the *Shakespeare in Performance* series also uses the New Cambridge edition. Thus the reader can either follow this account of the play alongside Bevington's edition with its explanatory and textual notes, or use Madelaine's, which gives details from past productions.

The Cambridge *Antony and Cleopatra* text is taken from the First Folio of Shakespeare's plays. This is the only authoritative text of the play. It had no Act or scene divisions – these have been added by later editors. The First Folio was produced in 1623 by printer and publisher William Jaggard and his son, and with the blessing – and probably the help – of the King's Men actors John Heminge and Henry Condell. They had performed with Shakespeare, and signed a dedicatory preface to the volume. Some of the plays included in the Folio were taken from single volumes – Quartos – of plays already published. Some were taken from Shakespeare's own drafts in various stages of development. Others were taken from the promptbooks used in the theatre. It is clear that the F1 copy of *Antony and Cleopatra* has not been produced from a promptbook, as there are a number of inconsistent entrances and exits in it, and named characters who have nothing to say. The prompt or book-keeper's job was to transcribe the text from the author's copy, and, like a modern stage manager, write into it stage directions and props used in production (his work in performance was to prompt the actors and make sure they entered on cue, and he made changes and corrections in his copy according to what happened in performance). Early editions of Shakespeare's plays based on promptbooks do not have many of the kinds of inconsistencies to be found in the Folio's *Antony and Cleopatra*, as the book-keeper would have corrected them. It is likely, then, to have been taken from Shakespeare's own papers – many scholars think from a good, late draft of the play or 'fair copy', though some have found enough mistakes and inconsistencies in it to suggest that the F1 *Antony and Cleopatra* is based on earlier drafts or 'foul papers'.

The modern editor has many decisions to make when producing

a modern-spelling edition of a 400-year-old play. Not only was Shakespeare's spelling of proper names and other words inconsistent, it was easy for the compositors – those responsible for typesetting the play – to misread certain letters in an author's handwriting, and they also made mistakes themselves. It is not, then, always clear to the editor which modern word to choose where meaning is unclear. The editor also has decisions to make about how lines of verse should be set out in a modern edition. Where Shakespeare writes in verse, he almost always uses the iambic pentameter, or blank verse. The five-stress lines of this metric form can be divided up amongst speakers, and by the time he came to write *Antony and Cleopatra*, Shakespeare was using it in complex and fluid ways. The compositors of the Folio did not, as many modern editors do, indent speeches to show where an iambic line is divided between speakers – for example here, when Cleopatra's question to Enobarbus completes a line of verse spoken by Antony, then Antony's speech finishes the iambic pentameter started by Enobarbus:

> ANTONY   Well, my good fellows, wait on me tonight:
> Scant not my cups, and make as much of me
> As when mine empire was your fellow too,
> And suffered my command.
> CLEOPATRA   What does he mean?
> ENOBARBUS   To make his followers weep.
> ANTONY   Tend me tonight.
>
> (IV.ii.21–5)

There are several occasions in *Antony and Cleopatra* where it is not clear if a character's line completes another's line of verse, or starts a new one. An example David Bevington gives is:

> MESSENGER   News, my good lord, from Rome.
> ANTONY   Grates me! The sum.
> CLEOPATRA   Nay, hear them Antony.
>
> (I.i.18–20)

If the editor decides that 'Grates me!' should complete the previous line, the text will read, as in the Riverside Shakespeare edition:

MESSENGER News, my good lord, from Rome.

ANTONY   Grates me! The sum.

CLEOPATRA Nay, hear them Antony.

Here, Antony attempts to cut off what might be a long speech concerning the news from Rome by completing the messenger's line of verse. If Antony's words remain unindented, as in Bevington's text, this interpretation still holds, but Cleopatra can also be seen, in continuing Antony's line, to be denying him that closure, wanting to draw out a subject that irritates him. Here is a good reason for using the New Cambridge text when considering the play as performance, even though the lengthy scholarly notes do not make for a convenient rehearsal edition. Where there are choices to be made as to how speeches fit the iambic pentameter, Bevington's decisions are based on theatrical logic. This is not to say that nothing can be gained by considering a broken line such as II.ii.30–40 – Antony and Caesar's awkward meeting – as an iambic pentameter. However, I would rather suggest that the actor who is trained in verse-speaking will remain aware of these rhythms and how they might inflect his delivery here, and does not need an awkward scansion imposed by the text.

Stage directions in all early modern play texts are minimal by more recent standards. There are, of course, no lengthy instructions as to the style or placing of scenery or furniture, as in later realist dramas, as Shakespeare's stage was a bare one with few props or large pieces. During the eighteenth century, editors of Shakespeare's plays attempted to give locations for each scene, a complex task in *Antony and Cleopatra*, whose action moves around the world so rapidly. Shakespeare simply would not have considered offering this information to the company performing his play. When we need to know where characters are meeting – for example, on whose territory the meeting between Antony and Caesar in Act II, scene ii, takes place – the dialogue will generally tell us: 'Welcome to Rome' (II.ii.30). Elsewhere, where the modern reader might feel obliged to pour over the play and notes trying to find out just where a particular battle might be taking place, the fact of a victory or a betrayal is more important than its exact location. Jacobean stage directions tend simply to tell us who enters and with what important prop – '*Enter Dercetus with the sword of Antony*' (V.i.3); in what symbolic formation – '*Enter Antony, Caesar, Octavia between them*' (II.iii); or whether together or separately – '*Enter Agrippa at one door, Enobarbus at another*' (III.ii). Even such minimal directions are not consistent, and the modern editor considers it part of his or her work to add to them and tidy them up. For example, though Shakespeare demands different entrance doors for Agrippa and Enobarbus in Act III, scene ii, there is no similar stage direction when Antony and Caesar enter for their parley in Act II, scene ii. David Bevington adds the directions in square brackets, as below:

> LEPIDUS   . . . Here comes the noble Antony.
>   *Enter* ANTONY *and* VENTIDIUS [*in conversation*]
> ENOBARBUS   And yonder Caesar.
>   *Enter* CAESAR, MAECENAS *and* AGRIPPA [*by another door, also in conversation*].
>   (II.ii.14–15)

In fact, it is clear from the text that follows that the two groups of men are 'in conversation', and from preceding dialogue between Lepidus and Enobarbus that this whole scene is to turn on a meeting about to happen, making it obvious that the two groups should enter from different doors. At the beginning of III.ii, the dialogue does not make separate entrances for Enobarbus and Agrippa explicit: they could be entering together in conversation, but for the stage directions in F1. However, the last time we have seen them has been in II.vii, at the feast on Pompey's galley. Between the two scenes is another, in a different location – III.i, Ventidius's bearing away of Pacorus's body. By making it clear at the opening of III.ii what the dialogue does not, Shakespeare shows that Enobarbus and Agrippa are not wandering in drunken camaraderie from the party at the galley – the night has passed, Caesar and Antony's men are separated once more.

Not all modern additions to the stage directions follow an obvious internal direction. Where a character's entrance is missing, for example, the editor is sometimes presented with a choice as to where it should come, and must shut down one theatrical possibility by choosing another (for example, Charmian's entrance in IV.iv, see p. 69). The exact line on or after which characters might kiss, for example, or shake hands, will alter their relationship as it is seen on stage. The choice of stage directions regarding the mechanics of Cleopatra's capture in the monument (F1 gives none) will produce a particular stage interpretation of the theatrical moment.

It is important to keep in mind, then, that the *Antony and Cleopatra* we see on the page and on the stage has been filtered through, indeed produced by, a number of minds and processes before it reaches us. Early conditions of performance and early printing practices, later staging and editing conventions, all make and re-make the play. This *Handbook* offers a range of interpretations that use and acknowledge these conditions of production; it aims to give the student and performer of the play useful ways in to his or her own readings.

2 *Commentary*

ACT I

Act I, scene i

Antony refuses to hear messengers from Rome and is taunted by Cleopatra.

1–17 Demetrius and Philo enter, in debate. Philo's first line is a negative response to something we imagine Demetrius may have spoken in Antony's defence. Even before we meet him, then, Antony is a subject of controversy. Philo's speech introduces the love affair upon which the plot turns, the play's recurring imagery of plenty and excess, its binaries of male/female, Roman/Egyptian. It typifies the attitude of many of the play's male characters towards Antony. According to the Romans in the play, Antony's relationship with Cleopatra reduces and emasculates him. This scene also introduces a dilemma that is at once thematic and theatrical: how can Antony the flawed lover of Cleopatra, and Antony the mytho-historical war-hero and epitome of masculinity, exist within the same figure? According to Philo he has failed to live up even to what his men at arms expect of him. Having turned his 'goodly eyes' from the battle-field, to gaze upon Cleopatra's 'tawny front', Antony has both burst his proper bounds and is newly imprisoned; he is not himself. Philo's once heroic Antony is now described as 'bellows' and 'fan', mere domestic objects at the service of Cleopatra's lust and the makers of boundless, airy sighs of love.

    A number of modern productions have included the audience in Philo's address. Though this flies in the face of a dramaturgy that deliberately opens the play with private conversation, addressing the audience here can give weight to Philo's disapproval. It gives him a direct and complicitous relationship with the spectator and creates a genuine dilemma for the audience, who may otherwise be swept away by the entrance of Cleopatra's court next. A Philo who comments directly on the action encourages us to watch ourselves watching, and puts us in a productive observational frame for the rest of the performance.

Our first sighting of the lovers is a public one. Whether raucous and drunken or a more ceremonious display, the procession of attendants, eunuchs and fans is an immediate visual contrast with the personal conversation that precedes it. How far Antony appears to be a 'strumpet's fool' will depend on his place and attitude in the train. He might indeed appear as a foolish hanger-on in this royal procession, an attendant alongside the ladies and eunuchs there to serve Cleopatra. He can also make his entrance as the double pillar of his and Cleopatra's world, a world that centres entirely upon their love, until messengers from Rome threaten to decentre this boundless universe of passion. The lovers appear delighted to display their private affections in public. However, it is not Cleopatra demanding excess here. She speaks of boundaries for love (l. 16), Antony of limitless affection (l. 17).

18–45   Enter, with a Roman messenger, the inconvenient fact of Antony's military commitments to Caesar and an infuriating reminder, for Cleopatra, of Antony's wife, Fulvia. In refusing to let the subject of Fulvia drop, Cleopatra could be seen as playfully provoking Antony to grandiose declarations, or the actress might read a needy insecurity into these lines. The pair might play the exchange as the kind of conversation they have had many times before, a playful rhetorical battle of flirtatious wit, or as an encounter that prefigures Cleopatra's later jealous tempers. Whatever decision is made about characterisation here, Antony and Cleopatra's dialogue must be contextualised in terms of its public nature. Cleopatra is happy to tease and humiliate Antony before her ladies, eunuchs and audience. The consciousness of performance and display that suffuses this play, particularly on Cleopatra's part, is introduced with a pleasing economy in this scene.

The scene sets the pattern of swift shifts from public to private moments and from moods of passionate joy to fury or irritation, the latter usually and celebratedly on the part of Cleopatra but here, interestingly, on Antony's. Antony's poetic expansiveness in whole blank-verse lines switches to an irritated abruptness as he completes the messenger's first line (ll. 18–19). This is the first of the many unfortunate messengers for which the play is noted, and he never gets to deliver his news, despite Cleopatra's ironic demands that Antony hear them (l. 20).

Cleopatra's tone can be playful or bitter as she taunts Antony with the 'angry' Fulvia and the 'scare-bearded' Caesar, who, she ironically insists, have the power to give her lover orders. Antony's 'How, my love?' suggests surprise at the outburst. However light or dark her irony, many recent productions have had the courtiers laugh at Cleopatra's pretended confusion as to whether Antony's orders come from Caesar or Fulvia (l. 30). Line 31 offers Cleopatra the opportunity to shift to a dignified anger mid-line, but I suggest that the speech's main purpose is victory in a battle for theatrical status. Cleopatra is 'Egypt's queen', Antony supposedly 'blushest' like someone who has forgotten his lines (ll. 31–2). He now attempts both to pacify Cleopatra and to return to the expansive, self-dramatising language of his opening exchange with her. His speech of lines 35–42 is a celebrated one; it establishes a concept central to the play, that of the glorious and mythic passion that overrides the mundane concerns of the 'dungy earth' (l. 37). Nevertheless, Cleopatra is able to undercut its grandiosity by calling him a fool (ll. 44–5).

45–57   The actor playing Antony can be allowed to regain ground in the status battle next, with a tone of good-humoured patronage. Though he appears to be wheedling at lines 42–8, he might speak of their 'sport tonight' as if pacifying a child, gently upbraiding his 'wrangling queen' with compliments; Cleopatra can be played as correspondingly calm as she leaves the stage. It is worth noting, however, that from line 20, when Antony attempts to dismiss the messengers and hear only 'the sum' of their news, until the lovers' exit at line 57, it is Cleopatra who forces all the changes in tone and pace in the dialogue, she who provokes the shifts and parries in the status battle between them. This is the scene that introduces her as the consummate performer and, as such, a consummately knowing and controlled performance is required, even if it is underpinned by jealous insecurity. Antony seems rattled by the whole encounter as he exits, snapping at the messenger.

58 to the end   After – or at the tail end of – the exit of the lovers and their train, Demetrius expresses shock that Caesar should be 'with Antonius prized so slight' (l. 58). Philo draws attention to the problem of mythologised selfhood in the play. The idea that when Antony is not Antony he falls short of being Antony (ll. 59–61) is a strange tautology, but one that reminds the audience to compare the Antony we have just seen in verbal combat with Cleopatra, with the Antony whose troops need him to be all soldier. Far from being pompously puritanical, the exchanges between Philo and Demetrius frame the scene with the interpretation that the outside world gives to Antony's actions. In some productions, Demetrius and the Roman messenger are conflated. It makes sense to have Philo speak his opening speech to a messenger of some status, and then for the latter to express both surprise at the rejection of his news (l. 58) and knowledge of how the 'common liar' speaks of Antony in Rome whence Philo-as-messenger has just come (ll. 63–4).

Act I, scene ii

Fortune-telling at Cleopatra's court; Antony receives the news that his wife is dead.

1–70   The scene opens amongst Cleopatra's servants and waiting women, at the Egyptian court. The first lines, spoken by Charmian, are the play's first prose passage and the scene as a whole plays fascinatingly with shifts from prose to verse, from comic playfulness to momentous predictions and news.

The opening impression is of a court in search of novelty and entertainment. Charmian's increasingly hyperbolic pleadings for Alexas to find the Soothsayer suggest that she might playfully hang upon Alexas or stop his way. Here we meet Enobarbus, Antony's follower and comrade at arms, who shows no interest in fortune-telling – for him a stay at such a court offers a chance of more down-to-earth entertainment, and he calls for a banquet and wine; the only reliable prediction he can make is of a drunken night. He is established as a man who is enjoying life at the Alexandrian court but remains humorously cynical about some of its pursuits.

The light-hearted fantasies of future husbands and children that Charmian wants the Soothsayer to offer her contrast starkly with the stern 'prescience' of the Soothsayer himself. The banter between Charmian, Iras and Alexas is full of jokes about fertility and cuckold-ing. Images of excess abound, particularly from Charmian (ll. 25–6); her teasing of Alexas (ll. 58–61) is a cruder echo of Cleopatra's under-mining of Antony. The Soothsayer gives an impression of stillness upon a stage full of skittish, flirtatious movement. The irony of his prediction that she will 'outlive the lady whom [she] serve[s]' (l. 30) is, of course, lost on Charmian. But she might be mildly disconcerted or disturbed by his determined lack of response to her levity. The tumbling prose rhythms of flirtatious joking are continually broken by the solemn blank verse of the Soothsayer's pronouncements, which Charmian expropriates to serve her own comedy turn, until the whole exchange is stopped abruptly by the entrance of Cleopatra.

70–82   The tone and pace change immediately; it is clear that Cleopatra is not in the mood for jokes, for though Charmian treats her queen playfully enough elsewhere in the play, and Enobarbus has been calling for wine to drink her health, their answers to her questions 'Saw you my lord? . . . Was he not here?' are subdued. Cleopatra stays on stage only long enough to precipitate this change in mood, ask Enobarbus to fetch Antony, and refuse to see her lover when he enters with a messenger. It is as though this time she wants to claim the power of leaving the stage for herself.

The scene begins with soothsaying, and this rapid entrance and exit of Cleopatra's is prescient too. She leaves on a whim and all follow her, like Antony at Actium. It is a moment that centres on notions of Cleopatra's presence, which the rhythmic structure of the lines produces for the actors. After the ebullient prose of the exchange with the Soothsayer, Cleopatra reduces the court to short, broken lines that attempt to pick up a blank verse rhythm but fail, as Cleopatra once more stops the flow of conversation with 'Was he not here?' She then shifts the scene back into iambic pentameter with the languid bitterness of lines 77–8.

Cleopatra has the court move about her to carry out her bidding, giving an order to Enobarbus and calling for Alexas in one line, then tops this show of queenly and theatrical status with a royal 'we' and a clearing of the stage (l. 82).

83–128 Antony enters, in conversation with a messenger, and the audience might feel somewhat relieved that Cleopatra has left: the messenger's first word is 'Fulvia', whose military manoeuvres he is reporting (l. 83). This is a different Antony from the one we have seen with Cleopatra: the firmness of purpose that Philo lamented in Act I, scene i, is fully in evidence. The messenger, who has bad news of fighting in Asia, is hesitant and faltering; Antony demands the truth of what has been said about the role his own absence has played in the military disasters, and finishes the sentence the messenger dare not speak. The actor playing Antony then has the opportunity to build to something of bitterness once he has demanded that the messenger 'Speak to me home; mince not the general tongue' (l. 101). Antony is aware that there is some truth in gossip about his neglect of the wars. He appears angry both at himself and at the world.

His speech of lines 101–7 ends in a textual crux, most editors emending the Folio's 'winds' to 'minds' in lines 105–7. It is an extended metaphor that can easily be cut without breaking the blank-verse line: Antony can demand that the messenger taunt his faults 'With such full licence as both truth and malice / Have power to utter' (ll. 104–5), then finish the line with 'Fare thee well awhile.' However, uncut, the lines give a dark wisdom to the speech, whose bitter overtones might otherwise blur the fact that Antony is admitting there is not just malicious gossip abroad: he has made mistakes. Keeping to 'winds' here not only makes sense in terms of soft winds supposedly being good for crops, but also recalls Midas's whispering grasses speaking his foolishness; if the grasses are still, and no news reaches us of our own mistakes, we are likely to reap weeds. On the other hand, the modern production company may wish to retain the

amendment 'minds', as it makes easier sense; it also fits with
Antony's sense that he is losing himself, in remaining with Cleopatra
(l. 113).

Antony dismisses the messenger and calls for news from Sicyon,
where he has left Fulvia, and there follows a short flurry of messen-
gers. These enter, then exit to find the one who can bring the news.
Alone on stage, Antony now determines to break 'These strong
Egyptian fetters', as if Cleopatra is a prison from which he must
escape: if he stays he will 'lose [him]self' (lines 112–13). When not in
Cleopatra's presence, then, Antony takes on something of the
Roman attitude to Egypt.

This is another of this scene's moments of stillness amidst flurries
of activity, the others provided by the Soothsayer and by Cleopatra's
entrance. Perhaps the question Antony asks the Sicyon messenger on
his entrance – 'What are you?' (l. 113) – sounds particularly stark only
to modern ears, but the exchange between them is by any standards
an unsettling one. The messenger does not answer Antony but cuts
across the niceties of greeting with the news of Fulvia's death (l. 114).

The actor playing Antony must now decide how this news is to be
taken. The key to the soliloquy that follows is in his relationship with
the audience. The speech begins as something of a confession to us.
Antony admits simply that he desired his wife's death. Then, after five
lines of musing upon how one wants what one can no longer have, it
is as though the vulnerability of the confessional soliloquy becomes
too much for him and he must move to action, to break from
Cleopatra. He appears unsettled by the paradoxical lack of control
brought about by a situation in which what he has desired has actually come about. Before calling Enobarbus to arrange a swift departure, he seems almost panicked by what else might happen in his
absence.

128 to the end   The exchange that follows is shot through with a
painful irony. Antony clearly wants to make a quick departure;
Enobarbus prevents it with his lengthy piece of comic prose, in
which he makes jokes at the expense of Cleopatra's performances
and puns on the sexual connotations of women 'dying', with a brief
but unsuccessful interruption by Antony at line 133.

When Antony blurts out a bitter 'Would I had never seen her!' (l. 147), Enobarbus demurs. There are many examples of his admiration for Cleopatra in the play and he clearly enjoys his time at her court. His exclamation to Antony (ll. 148–50) has been cited as an example of the colonialist elision of the exotic female and the exotic land, with Antony depicted as a traveller collecting celebrated sights of which to tell on his return. This is convincing, but does not mean that Enobarbus should be played as coarsely dismissive of Cleopatra here, despite the misogyny of lines 134–6. He is a figure just as capable of speaking his mind to women as to men, so while, here with Antony, his speeches smack of soldierly machismo and colonialist objectification, later we will see a movingly frank relationship with Cleopatra emerging.

Once again in this scene, and even more dramatically, a section of tumbling comic prose is stopped short by an exchange of short sentences. The audience, knowing the news of Fulvia's death, has been waiting for this. Antony answers Enobarbus's jokes about the wonderful piece of work that is Cleopatra with the stark statement, 'Fulvia is dead.' The almost comic awkwardness of the exchange as Antony has to repeat himself in the face of Enobarbus's shock or incredulity reads as startlingly naturalistic (ll. 151–5).

Several productions have broken the tension here with laughter from the two men, as if Antony is forced to admit that Fulvia's death is what he has wanted all along. However, though his response to Enobarbus's somewhat tasteless exhortation at line 156 is not necessarily stern and unsympathetic, Antony has shown us that his feelings about his wife and his desire to be rid of her are guiltily mixed. The release and relief of laughter do not seem to me to be appropriate here, unless underpinned with nervousness or embarrassment at being seen to laugh in our presence at such a time. Eventually, after all, Antony puts a stop to Enobarbus's levity (l. 169) – and returns to organising their departure. The last of Antony's speeches in the scene precipitates their exit; the sentences begin to run over the blank-verse lines, ending in the summation that the situation must not be allowed to get any worse (ll. 185–7). Antony demands that Enobarbus tell of 'our quick remove from hence' (l. 189) and Enobarbus can only reply 'I shall do't' (l. 189), punctuating the scene and suggesting a hasty departure from the stage and from Egypt.

Act I, scene iii

Antony's departure.

Having heard from Enobarbus of the ways in which Cleopatra can manipulate Antony, with tears like storms and sorrows like dying, we now see her in action. The events of Act I, scene iii, clearly occur soon after the previous scene: when Cleopatra opens with 'Where is he?' we are presumably to imagine Antony giving orders for packing.

1–12 At this point in the play, we have already observed a brief example of Cleopatra's tactics in love, when she calls for Antony then refuses to 'look upon him' (I.ii.82). Now she makes these tactics explicit to Alexas (ll. 3–5). Both Alexas and Charmian are party to her secrets here. Charmian appears particularly familiar with Cleopatra: not impressed by her mistress's strategies, she proposes a more submissive plan (l. 10). Cleopatra dismisses such temerity, and an audience that knows the lovers' fate knows that Cleopatra's way will succeed in binding Antony to her in love, but will also sever the pair in death. However, it is difficult to imagine anyone applauding Charmian's advice wholeheartedly. The audience know they are about to witness a skilled piece of play-acting, and though we may well doubt the ethics of this mode of 'enforcing' love, we know that the plot and our pleasure in the scene are dependent on it.

13–73 The swift shift from the acknowledgment of play-acting (l. 13) to the play-acting itself before Antony (l. 15), makes for a comic beginning to the lovers' exchange here. However, in this scene there is undoubtedly the potential for real fury behind some of Cleopatra's words. Having threatened to faint, she turns on Antony, launching at him with the unanswerable argument that he cannot possibly be '[hers] and true' when 'false to Fulvia' (ll. 27–9). Refusing him the chance of equal eloquence (l. 32), she moves swiftly from denying that his vows could possibly mean anything, to immortalising them in the celebrated lines 35–7. As we have seen, Antony is particularly fond of mythologising this relationship in language, so these are clever tactics, even if spoken with utter sincerity.

Antony is left spluttering short lines of attempted interruption throughout the exchange of lines 13 to 41. One imagines Cleopatra having command of the stage space here, either moving about it at will while Antony is left adrift in a centre-stage 'authority position' that fails to endow him with any authority, or standing and declaiming while Antony tries different physical as well as vocal means to interrupt. As in Act I, scene ii, Antony is once more obliged to listen to speeches that are a most unfitting prologue to the announcement of his wife's death.

Eventually, Antony does get a reasonably lengthy speech in edgeways, and manages to regain some of the purposeful expository rhythm and tone of his last speech to Enobarbus. He lays before Cleopatra all the reasons for leaving, crowning his argument with Fulvia's death. The fact that he does not blurt out his news to silence Cleopatra, but caps his speech with it, suggests a deliberate attempt to regain control of the exchange here.

Cleopatra's first reaction to the death of her rival contains an indication of the way in which she has dramatised her relations with Antony (ll. 57–8). Fulvia, it appears, is not human but a symbol, an immortal sign of Antony's ultimate unattainability. Once Cleopatra has accepted the truth, she reverts once more to her insistence that the way in which Antony treats Fulvia shadows her own fate; she demands to see Antony's tears for Fulvia, then tries the fainting act again (l. 71). Cleopatra's order to Charmian to cut her lace points to the fact that Shakespeare's first Cleopatra would have worn Jacobean costume rather than robes more naturalistically appropriate to the ancient world. It almost seems worth adapting the costume to accommodate this line, as it is such a strong visual example of the way in which the world of Cleopatra's court revolves around her. Charmian must run to her to start adjusting her clothing, then is almost instantly sent away at lines 72–3; Cleopatra can assume that everyone at court – at least when they are actually in her presence – will act as though they believe in her shows of instant sickness and recovery. The actress playing her might want to motivate the queen by deciding that in these moments of 'playing', Cleopatra sometimes believes herself. The two lines following the command to Charmian are appropriately ambiguous: 'I am quickly ill and well; / So Antony loves' can mean that Antony's love and withdrawal of it determine her state of health; the lines can also read as a taunt – her state of health is as changeable as Antony.

73 to the end   In the accusations that follow, Antony is once more talked into a corner from which it is impossible to escape. He attempts to make a legal scene of the exchange, in which his defence is clear (ll. 73–5). She makes a theatre piece of his efforts, making fun of his weak integrity (ll. 76–85) and drawing Charmian into the joke by criticising his acting progress. As in Act I, scene i, Cleopatra *shows* Antony to her ladies and the audience, putting herself in that highest of theatrical status positions, that of the knowing onlooker. Antony's only recourse is to threaten to leave the stage.

Rather than regard it as an example of outrageous hypocrisy on the part of this player queen, it is productive to read this passage as a point in the play where notions of performance are most clearly foregrounded. Cleopatra, the notoriously wayward, capricious, dissembling female, here suggests that Antony's masculine, heroic, Roman world might also be in some ways a performed one.

As soon as Antony threatens to leave Cleopatra without her audience, she ceases her taunting, and it is difficult to describe her next dialogic gambit as a manipulative tactic, as it seems so sincere. She stops him with a request for 'one word' (l. 87), and though more words than that certainly follow, they are moving in their simplicity and their seeming lack of the performed control central to the previous exchange (ll. 87–92).

The audience may feel that they have been permitted a genuine glimpse of vulnerability at 'O my oblivion is a very Antony / And I am all forgotten (ll. 90–92). Another little joke on Antony's forgetfulness can still be marked without losing the sincerity of the moment.

Antony, however, is not inclined to credit this shift in mood with authenticity, and there is the opportunity for a look to the audience here as he undermines the effect of her words by accusing her of 'idleness' (l. 93). This is his chance to turn the tables on Cleopatra, to show her performance to us, as she has done to his own detriment. Her next speech appears to soften him, however. She plays with his word 'idleness', turning it to her own advantage, and then appears to do something rather risky. She actually draws Antony's attention to her own play-acting and manipulations, and gives Antony the power of the audience, to approve or disapprove of them (ll. 97–8). She owns up to the scene's extraordinary displays, and then declares that they have only been for him.

So, this exchange can be offered with sincerity by the actress playing Cleopatra – but the audience, like Antony, will never be sure what to believe. In her final formal farewell she abandons the vulnerable hesitancy of lines 86–91. She now gives such a conventional performance of humility that, as she has had to admit defeat and Antony is going no matter what she says, one wonders whether she has made a conscious decision to play the virtuous lady wishing victory to her lord (l. 100). Whether the actress finds it useful to think of this as another conscious performance or not, it seems almost to work as a tactic. Antony does leave, but his parting lines seem full of longing to stay, and his last 'Away!' (l. 105) appears to be his way of forcing himself to leave the stage.

Act I, scene iv

Caesar and Lepidus discuss Antony.

1–33   After three scenes at the Egyptian court, we are torn away, like Antony, to a male terrain of battle reports and strict disapproval of the world we have just left. This is Octavius Caesar's Rome, and here he is in conversation with the third of the triumvirate, Lepidus. Cleopatra still dominates the opening of the scene, in that her court and Antony's activities there are at the centre of the men's conversation. However, these Roman generals, Caesar in particular, do not appear to have been seduced by ideas of the exotic decadence of her court. Instead Caesar purports to find it repellent in its excesses, particularly where they have infected Antony. This is a scene that supports the notion of a thematic divide in the play: that between Rome and Egypt, with Rome as masculine, functional, morally upright, Egypt as its exotic, unpredictable feminine other. The designer has to decide how far to reflect this in the décor, and there has been a preponderance, in production, of stark greys, whites and blues to represent Rome and to contrast with the rich warmth of Alexandria.

This scene, together with the banquet on the galley (II.vii), is the source of many stage interpretations of Caesar as a repressed figure, cold and formal. In his first speech, he refers to himself in the third person. His critique of Antony's life at Cleopatra's court centres upon how its power to emasculate Antony (ll. 5–7). Lepidus is introduced to us as the peacemaker, more inclined to hope that Antony's qualities can hardly all have been dissipated, but Caesar dismisses him as 'too indulgent' (l. 16). Recalling Hamlet in the 'closet scene', describing at length to his mother what she must stop doing with his uncle, Caesar is given a sentence that stretches over six lines, painting in sensual detail what Antony might be up to – tumbling on Cleopatra's bed, enjoying the company of 'knaves that smell of sweat' (l. 21). Caesar's central argument is that this would all be bad enough, did Antony not have responsibilities on the battlefield. But he takes a while getting to the point. His speeches are not expository: the audience has had plenty of time to see what Antony has been doing. The lines might lead the modern actor to consider repression as a key to the characterisation of Octavius Caesar and to speculate as to whether beneath his evident desire for conquering and control there lies a need to control his own desires. Others have read him as genuinely asexual and emotionless, focused entirely on order and control and disgusted at Antony's lack of it. Yet another possible focus is Octavius's past relationship with Antony: the anger of these speeches might reflect Octavius's intense disappointment in the older man he once admired.

There is no doubt that control of one sort or another is the key to playing Caesar, and his control of the stage space and of other figures on stage is the most productive place to start a reading of this character. A contrast in the way the stage space is used by the actors in the Egyptian and Roman courts will be telling. The F1 stage direction has Caesar and Lepidus entering with 'their train' rather than found in intimate conversation, and it is unsurprising that the direction is sometimes ignored in modern productions. There is not the clear sense one has at Cleopatra's court of the 'train' being used as an on-stage audience by the central characters. However, the presence of attendants makes Caesar's anger at Antony a matter of public pronouncement rather than a private word in Lepidus's ear, and the presence of other Romans in the scene necessitates some decisions as to how they are to react to Octavius's disgusted description of the Alexandrian revels. Might they, like Enobarbus, quite enjoy the idea of some time off at Cleopatra's court? Caesar might demonstrate status and control by ignoring the 'train' entirely, or he might be a Caesar who knows how to make his men laugh at the image of an effeminate Antony. The presence of attendants could also result in a Lepidus who is keen that his fellow triumvir should not condemn their absent third too harshly in public. The speeches do not lend themselves to a low-voiced mutter. The formality of the opening first-person plural, the quality of announcement at 'This is the news' (l. 3), and the considered linguistic complexity and conventional morality of lines 8–10 suggest that Caesar wants all present to hear his condemnation of Antony.

If Caesar dominates the stage space with his voice, it is then necessary to decide how far that command is supported or undermined by his movements. The words of his second speech might suggest an imperfect control of temper, and the actor might choose to pace the stage with some degree of agitation. This will suggest a Caesar emotionally moved, in contrast to the calculating fascist some productions have made of him. He might as justifiably remain still and stern, in which case the sensuality of lines 15–20 may acquire a calmer, more contemptuous ring.

34 to the end   A messenger enters with news from the front. Pompey, the rival of the triumvirate, is, it seems, a more popular man than Caesar (lines 37–8), and it is significant that Caesar expresses no surprise (l. 44). Though he begins his explanation of the faithlessness of men with a measured logic (l. 41), his final image of the common people suggests contempt, even revulsion (ll. 44–7). Again, here is Caesar expressing an attitude that the modern production company might associate with fastidiousness or fascism. After the next piece of bad news from the war, the focus of the scene swiftly returns to Antony, as Caesar compares the 'lascivious wassails' (l. 56) of life in Egypt with the absent General's previous feats of endurance as a soldier. Again, Caesar's words are extraordinarily visceral. He describes with seeming revulsion Antony's pleasures; he tells, with a strange nostalgic fury, of the patience with which Antony has endured the most revolting hardships (ll. 62–9). After this lengthy and startling description, Lepidus is given only one short sentence – ''Tis pity of him' (l. 73) – as if silenced by the force of the tale.

The scene now moves to the pragmatic needs of war, and the two men confirm the tasks to be undertaken, and leave the stage. Caesar's farewell has a touch of dramatic irony about it: Lepidus asks that his comrade should tell him any news he might obtain 'of stirs abroad' (l. 84) and Caesar replies that he should not doubt it (l. 86). Lepidus will have much reason to doubt the trustworthiness of Caesar's 'bonds' of soldierly friendship as the plot progresses.

Act I, scene v

Cleopatra pines for Antony.

1–35 The brisk and business-like exit of the Roman Generals could not be more different in pace from the action that follows. This is Cleopatra's court at its most languid. The last lines of the previous scene have all been concerned with what is to be done, and Act I, scene iv, as a whole gives an impression of urgency: victory will slip away if action is not taken quickly to stem the tide of defection to Pompey. Here, in contrast, there is too much time with nothing to fill it: Cleopatra calls for the sleeping drug mandragora to kill the time of Antony's absence (ll. 3–5). The comic exchange with the eunuch, Mardian (ll. 9–19), is laden with obvious sexual innuendo, as is the image of the 'happy horse' that bears the weight of Antony when Cleopatra does not (l. 22). Cleopatra appears fully aware that she is enjoying wallowing in misery, feeding herself deliberately with the 'delicious poison' of Antony's memory (l. 28), and the opening has suggested to many directors a scene spent lying about the stage, eating and drinking.

The image of Cleopatra eating and being eaten is strong in her speech of lines 18–35. Here, at the end an Act full of dramatic irony and foretelling, the means by which the Egyptian queen finally takes her life is clearly prefigured in the close proximity of the 'serpent of old Nile' (l. 26) to the reference to poison (ll. 27–8). Cleopatra goes on to describe how she has been 'a morsel' for Julius Caesar (l. 32), and the image – the whole speech in fact – gives Cleopatra a paradoxical strength. To be someone's morsel, an insignificant object of consumption, surely means weakness and submission. However, the tone of this speech is a mix of self-congratulation and ironic self-knowledge, as Cleopatra draws attention to the colour and age of her skin as it is now, and recalls the roles she has played in the lives of great men. She may have been a mere 'morsel' but her looks have had the power to make a Pompey 'die with looking on his life' (l. 35).

It should be noted that I.v.29–30 contain the only direct description of what Cleopatra looks like, and it is a description spoken by Cleopatra herself. Much speculation has turned, on these lines, as to the age and race of the Cleopatra that Shakespeare and the early modern period might have imagined. Modern spectators will obviously read the speech according to the age and race of the actress on the stage. The reference to 'Phoebus' amorous pinches black' may or may not be a direct reference to Cleopatra's race (though I am convinced by broader arguments about her colonialised racial otherness in the play as a whole). The point of the description in theatrical terms is to draw the audience further in to the world of this contradictory figure; it shows that she is able to acknowledge the toll time has taken upon her and at the same time revel in the life she has led. The sun has made her progressively and unfashionably black – but it is a blackness that shows that even the sun has been in love with her.

36–70   Alexas enters, and Cleopatra finds in him another excuse to mention her lover before the court: the poor attendant is greeted with the fact that he is disappointingly unlike Antony. Some of the 'medicine' that is Antony has, Cleopatra declares, rubbed off on Alexas however (ll. 37–8), and this suggestion of recovery can be taken as a signal to change the pace of the scene at this point, from languid musing to something more lively. Antony's message to Cleopatra, accompanied by a pearl, is expansive and grandiose. Alexas paints a heroic picture of the General vowing to make Cleopatra mistress of all the East as he mounts a whinnying horse.

Antony's reported mood pleases the queen, though the 'well-divided disposition' (l. 56) which determines not to lower his men's morale by seeming sad is not one that he maintains to the end of the play (see Act IV, scene ii). Her determination to read every tiny piece of information to her own advantage is comical, as is Alexas's bafflement at the number of messages the queen sends to Antony (l. 66). Cleopatra is as hyperbolic and self-dramatising in speaking of her love in this scene as ever Antony could wish.

70 to the end   The scene ends with an exchange between Cleopatra and Charmian, and it seems Charmian is far from afraid to tease and goad her mistress. Charmian's praise of Caesar provokes violent language from the queen but it would be fair to assume the banter is nevertheless good natured, as Charmian continues in it so determinedly. The last speech begins with the wry recollection of her 'salad days' (l. 76) – yet another reference to food in this scene – and ends with the disturbing assertion that Antony will receive from her a letter every day or she will 'unpeople Egypt' (l. 81). There is a range of possibilities for the delivery of this line. It can be seen as a final stamp of Cleopatra's authority on a scene that has perhaps contained one joke at her expense too many for her liking. It can be thrown away, as if the death of her people were nothing to such a figure of power. It can be read as a defiant assertion, in the face of Alexas's bewilderment that she sends so many letters, that Antony is entirely central to her life and being. However it is spoken, the line cannot help but remind us of the power Cleopatra wields, and the ways in which the world might suffer as a result of the personal whims and quarrels of two such leaders.

ACT II

Act II, scene i

Pompey and his men discuss battle tactics.

There has been a long tradition of cutting the character of Pompey altogether from *Antony and Cleopatra*. Dryden, Kemble, Chatterton,

Asche and Nunn cut all references to him, as did Michael Attenborough in 2002 and Braham Murray in 2005. This has led to some creative reworking of the galley party of Act II, scene vii, or its removal altogether. Cutting this first Pompey scene can certainly quicken the pace of the developing plot at this point in the play. What we lose if it goes, however, is a sense that the plot is quickening for the warring generals themselves. The opening direction in F1 is 'Enter Pompey, Menecrates and Menas in a warlike manner' and the immediate impression is that there is no time to lose for the triumvirate: war continues as they make their plans and their enemies are gaining news of their actions.

1–27   Pompey begins the scene in conversation with Menas and Menecrates, though most editors give Menecrates no lines. The fact that his confederates are 'notorious pirates' (I.iv.49) has led a number of productions to interpret Pompey as a blunt, rough figure, but I suggest below that he is also as subtle a judge of character as any of the triumvirate.

Pompey is confident that he will 'do well' in the continuing wars, particularly while Antony, he thinks, 'in Egypt sits at dinner'; Menas is more circumspect as to whether the gods will support their action and has heard that 'Caesar and Lepidus / Are in the field.' Pompey's next speech slows the action completely. Recollecting what Antony is up to in Egypt draws him into Cleopatra's world of 'feasts' and 'Epicurean cooks' (ll. 23–4). Once more the imagery of food fills the lines, and if it were not for Varrius puncturing the atmosphere with his message that Antony is nearly at Rome, one could imagine a 'Lethe'd dullness' preventing Pompey from getting to battle at all. Cleopatra can command the stage even when she is not present, slowing the action of the men who are drawn into speaking of her.

27 to the end   Pompey is surprised at Varrius's message that Antony has stirred from Egypt, and he is prompted to action. His last couplet is a determined rhyming one. Whether the triumvirate will unite in enmity towards him is in the lap of the gods and he appears stoical and pragmatic at lines 51–2. The men leave, presumably in the same 'warlike manner' in which they came, and one has the impression of a

scene that might have been a purposeful walk over the stage had it
not been for the stasis created by Pompey's speech on Cleopatra's
powers.

Act II, scene ii

The triumvirate parley; Antony's marriage to Octavia is arranged.

1–14   The energy that drives the scene's opening clearly belongs to
Lepidus, as he anxiously attempts to persuade Enobarbus to help him
keep the peace between Antony and Caesar. Lepidus urges
Enobarbus to 'entreat' Antony 'To soft and gentle speech' (l. 3), and a
low voice is appropriate for Lepidus here, an urgent stage whisper to
contrast with Enobarbus's honest insistence that he will ask Antony
to do nothing but 'answer like himself'.

14–30   Antony and Ventidius enter at one side of the stage, Caesar,
Maecenas and Agrippa at another, both groups in private conversation. Lepidus begins the difficult task of bringing the supposed allies
together with a formal speech, once more using volume as a central
motif (ll. 22–4). Lepidus's role as peacemaker has already been introduced with his defence of Antony in Act I, scene iv; here he is
concerned above all with the appearance – or perhaps the sound – of
accord, no matter the difficulty of the subject to be debated (l. 26).
Antony appears kindly in his response to Lepidus here, sensitive,
perhaps, to his anxiety, and complimenting him on his speech. His
compliment is rather an ominous one, though: 'Were we before our
armies, and to fight, / I should do thus' he says, suggesting (though
the actor must decide whether consciously) that it is a fight, not a
discussion, that might ensue.

30–90   There follows a wonderfully economical demonstration of
the tension between Caesar and Antony, as they decide which of
them should first be seated (ll. 30–4). Caesar is gracious with his
'Welcome to Rome', but can also be seen as laying claim to territory
with the line. When Antony thanks him, Caesar beckons his comrade
to 'Sit', but Antony refuses and with a similarly guarded politeness

answers 'Sit sir.' Caesar's 'Nay then' suggests that he gives in and sits first, but not without some degree of suppressed exasperation.

The meeting does not proceed as Lepidus would wish. Antony's opening gambit is that Caesar has taken 'things ill which are not so, / Or being concern you not' (ll. 35–6), and five lines later Caesar takes up the word 'concern', denying that he would be offended at trivial matters. The repeated verb suggests a tension at the outset of the debate between Caesar and Antony, as if each aims to undermine his supposed ally with words, whilst not wishing to be the one who openly begins an argument. Rather than accusing Antony directly of 'practis[ing] on [his] state' (l. 45), Caesar phrases his next speech in the conditional tense, and Antony jumps on his accusation (l. 46), almost blowing aside the veil of politeness and demanding that subtexts be brought to the surface. Caesar and Antony continue to debate Antony's role in the battles begun by his wife and brother, each man taking up words from the other's argument, playing on 'patch' (ll. 58, 62) and 'wife' (ll. 70, 71). Antony blames his brother, his wife and his hangover for the troubles caused to Caesar. He clearly wants to create a more light-hearted atmosphere, but the tension between them increases to the point where Caesar goes so far as to accuse Antony of breaking his word. At a slur from one of the triumvirate on another's honour, Lepidus has to intervene, keen once more to quieten the argument, with a 'Soft, Caesar!' (l. 90).

91–117 Antony appears ominously calm at this insult, determined that Caesar should be allowed to make his accusation, as it is such a serious one. At two points in this scarcely veiled battle of words, Antony suggests that the actions that have offended Caesar have been caused by his not being 'himself' while at Cleopatra's court. He has excused his past abruptness towards Caesar's messenger with what amounts to the excuse of a hangover; he now claims that he has 'neglected' rather than 'denied' sending Caesar promised arms, 'when poisoned hours had bound me up / From my own knowledge' (ll. 96–8). It seems that it is not only Antony's followers who see Cleopatra as an influence who draws him away from his true self, but Antony himself. Both Antony and Cleopatra, then, shift their loyalties according to their company.

Lepidus and Maecenas are keen to accept Antony's half-apologies for his neglect of their wars, Maecenas recalling the 'present need' that should reunite the triumvirate (l. 108), a tactful attempt to smooth over the conflict. Enobarbus, however, clearly considers the great men's negotiations nothing but false politeness, and breaks the formality of the blank verse here by translating Maecenas' speech in a hilarious piece of tactless prose (ll. 110–13). The humour of the moment is heightened by the fact that this follows a line from Lepidus, who seems relieved at this point that everything is going so well. Though clearly close to Enobarbus elsewhere in the play, Antony now pulls rank (l. 114). Enobarbus's interruption recalls the silent attendants that the production company can have enter with Caesar and Lepidus in Act I, scene iv – Enobarbus's abrupt honesty contrasts humorously with their decorous silence.

118–182   Caesar is not so willing to dismiss Enobarbus's interruption, although he does not like 'the manner of his speech'. Caesar's desire to resolve differences between himself and Antony provokes Agrippa's suggestion that Antony marry Caesar's sister Octavia. The suggestion emerges from a tense little exchange, in which Cleopatra is mentioned by Caesar with what seems like a deliberately ironic tactlessness (ll. 128–30). Agrippa relieves the tension somewhat by putting forward his plan. In contrast to Enobarbus, Agrippa bides his time, asks permission to speak, leads tactfully up to his suggestion with persuasive infinitives (ll. 133–5), follows it up with formal reasoning then apologises (by way of mentioning that, unlike Enobarbus, he has considered his speech carefully and dutifully). Agrippa's plan is followed by an exchange similar to the terse debate over who will first be seated, as Antony asks Caesar to give his opinion of the marriage plan and Caesar insists Antony speak first.

The modern actress seeking for clues in the text for how Octavia is regarded by other characters in the play will find little to help her in Agrippa's praise of her here. Her beauty is defined by the 'best of men' that she deserves for a husband; her 'virtue' and her 'general graces' must speak for themselves. Her function is to ensure peace between the Generals, to make them brothers. Antony appears to need no persuasion to the marriage once he hears Agrippa has

Caesar's backing, and having shaken hands on the deal, the men soon return to discussion of Pompey's challenges by sea and by land. It is Antony who changes the subject here, perhaps with a sense of discomfort regarding what he has just agreed to. It is not only a modern audience who would doubt the success of the marriage, especially given that its discussion is followed so quickly by Enobarbus's celebrated description of Cleopatra's barge on the Cydnus. Octavia is treated here as a function of male relations, whilst Cleopatra surpasses and overrides them.

The actor playing Antony must decide how to play his acceptance of Octavia – whether, in the moment, he is pleased with the scheme, or whether his thoughts are with Cleopatra and he realises that he has been backed into a corner. It is interesting that few critics have noted a Cleopatra-like tendency to make decisions according to the interests of the moment here.

183–94 The triumvirate leave to 'view' Octavia, and the tense formality of the scene thus far disappears with them. There is an instant change of mood and energy as Enobarbus, Agrippa and Maecenas exchange the hearty greetings that the presence of their superiors had not permitted. The joys of feasting in Egypt are straightaway the subject and Enobarbus clearly relishes being able to top the rumours of Cleopatra's hospitality with the yet more excessive truth.

195–228 Enobarbus's lines describing Cleopatra's grand, floating parade down the Cydnus are amongst the best known in the play. They have, of course, inspired much in the way of extravagant design, particularly in film and late Victorian production. The modern theatre has been more inclined to recognise that if Cleopatra beggars Enobarbus's description here, the description itself renders excessive and unnecessary any attempt to reproduce it physically. It is clear that Enobarbus relishes taking the stage here, and Agrippa's responses (ll. 215, 228) show that the former has an open-mouthed audience. Direct, blunt and caustic elsewhere, Enobarbus shows a real admiration for Cleopatra here and the actor should not be concerned that the rough soldier's speech is too far transformed for consistency of character to hold. The actor might motivate the speech with real admiration for Cleopatra, or convey Enobarbus's desire to show his friends that the marriage with Octavia will surely fail in the face of this level of seduction. In the end, though, he must simply enjoy Shakespeare's adaptation of Plutarch and let Cleopatra work a transformation on Enobarbus, as she did on the people and the air around her. The description of Antony sitting alone in the market place (ll. 224–8) is, at any rate, at one with Enobarbus's dry humour.

229–38   This exchange between Enobarbus and Agrippa shifts the mood of the scene from awed wonder to macho banter – but it is banter very much at the expense of the men in Cleopatra's life rather than at hers. The description of Antony's excessive 'barber[ing]' conjures the image of an Antony effeminised by Cleopatra, recalling Sampson's weakness when shorn by Delilah. Cleopatra is once more portrayed as food for her lovers, but it is food for which Antony 'pays with his heart'. Agrippa's image of ploughing and cropping (l. 238) puts Julius Caesar in a dominant sexual position, but the image follows a line that suggests Cleopatra has emasculated even this legendary war hero (l. 237); putting one's sword to bed has a more literal as well as a sexual meaning.

239 to the end   Enobarbus's descriptions of Cleopatra in this scene are as remarkable in their variety as the queen is said to be. Having set her up as an awe-inspiring dramatic construction of royal and sexual power, here he has her hopping through the streets like a breathless little girl – and yet she is powerful even in a moment such as this (ll. 239–42). The short-stopped abruptness of Enobarbus's rebuke to Maecenas might be spoken with an incredulous irritation (l. 244), that after this whole exchange, the Roman still believes Antony might leave Cleopatra. Octavia's 'Beauty, wisdom' and particularly her 'modesty' (l. 250) seem rather feeble virtues to pit against the infinite variety that age cannot whither, and Enobarbus knows it. The actors playing Agrippa and Maecenas must decide whether they will leave the stage still hopeful that Maecenas's marriage plan will prove successful, or whether Maecenas's tone should give away a consciousness of the bathos of his lines at 250–2.

Act II, scene iii

Antony and Octavia; Antony and the Soothsayer.

1–9 This is the first of only two scenes in which we see Antony with Octavia, and the moment is a short one. The F1 direction has Octavia entering, symbolically, between her husband and her brother. Though Antony can be played as kindly, even affectionate, the contrast between this exchange and those with Cleopatra could not be clearer. Where Antony's first two lines to Cleopatra claim that their love is boundless (I.i.15–17), here the language is of limits and rules (ll. 6–7). Antony's plea to Octavia that she should not judge him according to the 'world's report' can be played with half a glance to Caesar, certainly one of the world's reporters on the subject of his decadence. The actress playing Octavia must decide how much and what kind of emotion her short speech and minimal farewell should reveal. The promise to be constantly in prayer for Antony in his absence (ll. 2–4) is a conventional enough utterance for the stock figure of a devoted wife with little psychological motivation for her devotion. The actress might choose to speak in subdued tones here, as if dutifully reciting what the wife of a great soldier should, whilst making the audience aware of her lack of agency in the marriage. She might, on the other hand, suggest a real love for Antony, and even display a consciousness of her symbolic position between the two men, looking from one to the other in the hope that they will remain on good terms.

10–31 The Soothsayer can be regarded as a solemn anti-clown, one who has licence to follow the central characters with a prescient commentary they may not want to hear. Just as in the Egyptian court of Act I, scene ii, the Soothsayer refuses to respond to flippancy. Antony addresses him with a disrespectful 'Sirrah' and uses him as a light-hearted means of turning the scene back to the subject of Egypt (l. 10) but the Soothsayer is as portentous as ever. Antony's next question (ll. 15–16) can be plausibly played as an attempt to keep the mood light, but the Soothsayer's solemn imperatives dominate the exchange, and Antony can only silence him by speaking to him as a servant, dismissing him with a message to Ventidius. The Romans – even Antony himself – often speak as though it is Cleopatra who emasculates Antony and prevents him from being his soldierly self; here Caesar becomes Antony's nemesis, supposedly overpowering Antony's otherwise noble spirit.

32 to the end   In a short soliloquy, full of the Soothsayer's fatalistic imagery of unlucky games, Antony's thoughts return to Egypt yet again. He is honest to us about his reasons for marrying, but the speech is nevertheless a slippery one. He appears to be using the Soothsayer's warning as an excuse to return to Egypt, in the presence of an audience who have just witnessed his promises to Octavia. His last instruction to Ventidius can be spoken with a degree of blustering relief that the soldier had entered and given him a less exposing ending to the scene than the admission that 'i'th' East [his] pleasure lies'.

Act II, scene iv

This short scene has often been cut, and might be regarded as spoiling a visual link between the lovers, as Antony leaves for the East, and Cleopatra enters and re-establishes that East on stage. The scene has its function, though, in once again establishing the difference in pace between the masculine world of travel and battles, here personified by Lepidus, Maecenas and Agrippa, and the world of leisure and stasis inhabited by Cleopatra. The exchange is all about haste and winning time, and flexible staging would allow Cleopatra's court to be entering at a suitably languid pace whilst the Romans cross the stage at the double.

Act II, scene v

Cleopatra is told of Antony's marriage.

1–15   Cleopatra's call for music and the sensual assonance of her first line takes us instantly back to Egypt. The scene begins in similar fashion to Act I, scene v, with the queen demanding music just as she called for mandragora, music that will exacerbate her languid melancholy and fill the theatre with the same. That mood has shifted somewhat from I.v, however, to a more restless dissatisfaction with stasis. Cleopatra wants music, then dismisses it, calls for billiards, then decides her arm aches, wants to go fishing, then forgets it as her mind drifts into metaphor, and Antony once more becomes her subject. The whole exchange, moreover, takes place between the women and Mardian the eunuch, with the obligatory joke at the expense of his inability to 'play' with Cleopatra. There can be no real activity of any kind when Antony is away, and where Cleopatra might spend the first speeches of I.v lying down amidst the debris of a feast, here a bored restlessness seems called for, which can only be combated by talk of Antony.

15–23   Charmian takes up the Antony theme, and the women's memories of the lovers' times together conjure images of a much more absorbed and active pleasure than the aborted entertainments of the scene itself. We have already seen Cleopatra's delight in and compulsion to performance, and in her description here it reaches its apotheosis, as she recalls the lovers swapping clothes and sword in bed. This erotic play-acting also, of course, epitomises the decadence of which Antony's comrades at arms despair – the ultimate unmanning of Antony at the hands of Cleopatra. The sense of play in this description gives the lie to Roman judgements, however. The delight Cleopatra takes in her memory of laughing Antony in and out of bed is captivating, and the remembered play of gender roles conjures a world of imaginative *jouissance* that can make the Roman world's sense of purpose appear self-important and two-dimensional.

23–75   All this non-penetrative play is followed by the entrance of a messenger and a swift change of imagery. The brutal sexual image in Cleopatra's first lines to the messenger (ll. 23–5) signals an end to the playful intimacy of the exchange with Charmian. The scene takes on an urgent pace, as Cleopatra stops dreaming of the past and demands to know what Antony is doing in the present. Those on stage in the scene up until now might touch and hang upon one another as they remember yet more intimate caresses. Now the dialogue between Cleopatra and the unfortunate messenger suggests a deadly game of cat and mouse, with the court clearing the floor in the face of the queen's rage at Antony's marriage. Cleopatra lavishes gold on the messenger in one moment, threatens to strike and kill him the next. This is often comical in performance, and there is a delicate balance to be found between real fury and a consciousness on the part of the queen that she is *playing* her fury to the messenger and to the court. If the production company have regarded her threat to 'unpeople Egypt' (I.v.81) as the expression of a cruel disregard for those beneath her, this might be a vicious scene, whether or not she is aware of the excesses of language in which she is indulging. It does work as a cartoon-like chase, though – one that might turn more serious on the news of the marriage to Octavia (l. 61), when classical references (l. 41) and playful promises of gold are replaced with a straightforward curse (l. 61). It is at the curse and the Folio direction 'strikes him down' that the sequence is potentially at its most serious. However, once Cleopatra has built up to the threat of throwing the messenger's eyeballs about, stewing him in brine and pickling him (ll. 65–7), the impact of the drawing of a knife (l. 74) is surely one of comic rather than terrifying climax for the audience. The switches from threat to pleading and back again are terrifying enough for the messenger, though, and he runs from the stage.

75–107   Cleopatra shows a consciousness of the ludicrous exhibition she has just made of herself, when the messenger has left the room. In reply to Charmian's rebuke (ll. 76–7) she is still inclined to self-dramatise, excusing her conduct in terms of great but uncontrollable acts of nature. On hearing that the messenger is afraid to return, however, she upbraids herself in what demands a quieter, self-confessional tone, and it is notable that she mentions the messenger's 'mean' position, which has allowed her so freely to vent her anger. A Cleopatra who has been basking in the assured admiration of her on- and off-stage audiences might now cast us something of a sheepish glance. Now the actress has to choose whether to terrify the messenger once again as Cleopatra speaks once more in classical hyperbole (ll. 97–9), or whether these lines are spoken in wretched grief. The messenger's asking for pardon rather then further frightened protest on his part points to the latter. Though Cleopatra's last words to him are another curse, her repetition of the question regarding Antony, 'He is married?' seems to suggest forlornness when followed by the image of a housewife for whom the messenger's Roman merchandise is too 'dear'. By the time the messenger has left the stage once more, Cleopatra's anger is spent and Charmian's call for 'patience' is as likely to be a response to tears as to more ranting.

108 to the end   Cleopatra's first lines, on the messenger's exit, prefigure her apparent betrayal of Antony for Caesar and the actress must decide how far to signal a consciousness of what will be. Her need for her women's physical and emotional support appears genuine here, as does the fainting that earlier in the play appeared performed and manipulative. She is enough in control to give explicit instructions regarding the report on Octavia's looks that she wants, but cannot bring herself to dismiss Antony from her thoughts and heart: she shifts from a determination to 'let him forever go' to an immediate retraction. She will allow Charmian no further words of comfort or exhortations to patience. The queen who usually parades, stalks or storms from the stage has to be helped from it by her attendant.

Act II, scene vi

A treaty is made between the triumvirate and Pompey.

1–8   The parley between Pompey and the triumvirate, witnessed by their assembled soldiery, begins with talk of hostages. The plan to talk before fighting is predicated on the fact that each side has no other choice, and despite the invitation with which this scene ends, tension between the warring parties underpins the scene.

8–23   Pompey's speech is guaranteed to stir up tension yet further, as he suggests some sympathy for the conspirators against Julius Caesar here. The back-story, whilst it will remind the audience of how the triumvirate was formed, serves no purpose from Pompey's perspective but to needle his rivals: he might as easily have told them he was out to avenge his father without drawing the comparison and defending the conspirators. Here is a key to how Pompey might be played: knowing and provocative, a past master at getting other men to condemn themselves.

23–48   Antony, Caesar and Lepidus clearly know that Pompey is attempting to intimidate them with his rhetoric and they demand that he return to the pragmatics of the territories and terms they have offered him. There is then something of a relaxation in the tension as Pompey reminds his enemies of how he has welcomed Antony's mother in Sicily. This speech (ll. 39–46) can be read as a tactic on Pompey's part to maintain some status whilst admitting that he intends to accept the offer, but the ensuing handshake at least bridges the physical distance between the men and is done, of course, in the presence of the armies of each.

48–73   The friendly gesture is undermined by Pompey's repeated reference to Cleopatra. Though he may well not know of Antony's marriage to Caesar's sister – it is news to his follower, Menas, as we will see – it can still be played as deliberate needling, especially when it comes to the reference to Cleopatra's past affair with Julius Caesar (ll. 70–2), which Pompey appears deliberately to bring up, only to pretend innocence by making Enobarbus finish the story. Enobarbus's attempt at tact here is comical: he short-circuits the tense little exchange between Pompey and Antony concerning what Pompey has 'heard' about Cleopatra's past doings (ll. 66–70) but then is almost tricked by Pompey into telling the tale of the 'mattress'.

73–83   It is Enobarbus's bluntness that reminds Pompey that they have met before, and indeed it is this bluntness that breaks the tension of the scene. Though Pompey is a master of the sly dig, he appears to enjoy straightforwardness when he meets it. The honest exchange of compliments on each man's prowess in battle is, for Enobarbus, entirely compatible with an open acknowledgement that he and Pompey are not friends, and the former tense pretence of camaraderie between his betters is swept away. Pompey's invitation to his galley seems genuine at this point in the scene, whereas had it emerged directly from his dialogue with the triumvirate, one might have suspected ulterior motives.

83 to the end   Once again, followers of the male protagonists are left to gossip about their doings when their betters have left the stage. This sequence begins with Menas expressing his distaste at Pompey's treaty (l. 84) and many modern editors mark his words as an aside. Clearly the line is not meant for Pompey to hear as he leaves, but I see no reason why Enobarbus should not hear it, as Menas expresses as much directly to him again at lines 104–5. The opening exchange between Menas and Enobarbus is abrupt and somewhat combative, a testing of the water between the two men, but once again Enobarbus breaks the tension and restores homosocial ease with his joke about the untrustworthiness of women. The conversation then turns to Cleopatra and it is clear Menas has not heard of the marriage to Octavia. At line 117 Menas speaks what the audience must have been thinking all along, and Enobarbus reveals that despite his role as 'considerate stone' during the brokering of the marriage, he has always thought it to be doomed. The exchange about Octavia's conversation – holy, cold and still – and Menas's approval of it as a desired quality in a wife is an interesting one to consider in terms of the position of women in Shakespeare's time. Menas praises conventional female passivity, whereas Enobarbus suggests that support for companionate marriage is equally current. For the actor playing Enobarbus, his affectionate but somewhat despairing knowledge of Antony is a key to his character here.

Act II, scene vii

The feast aboard Pompey's galley.

This scene of Roman revels is in marked contrast to the pictures Enobarbus has painted of the Egyptian court, which, though excessive, appears by comparison genuinely generous in its excess. Pompey's banquet is marked by Menas's aborted assassination plot, and a sense that there is never a time in the Roman world when being off one's guard is advisable.

1–15   The servants who enter with the banquet here set the scene with their commentary on Lepidus's drunkenness, indicating that the revels have already been going on for some time. They foreshadow Lepidus's fate and regard him as the weakest of the three, whether drunk or no. '*Music plays*' from the beginning of the scene, which presumably ripens to something more raucous for the 'Egyptian Bacchanals' later.

16–48   Lepidus is a comical and rather endearing drunk, clearly wide-eyed at Antony's description of things Egyptian. Lines 25–6 will ring true to anyone who has had to sit at a bar listening to a drunken 'expert'.

It is significant that Antony is still harping on Egypt and its oozing fertility. Caesar overhears this exchange, commenting somewhat contemptuously at Lepidus's easy acceptance of Antony's comic description of the crocodile. The actor playing Caesar might consider whether part of his irritation at the drunkenness around him stems from suspicion at Antony's continuing preoccupation with the East. Pompey continues to enjoy capitalising on his enemies' weaknesses, plying Lepidus with more drink in the guise of the friendly host. He is clearly enjoying the role, and waves Menas away when he attempts to draw him aside.

49–77   Menas eventually manages to gain Pompey's attention for his plot to betray the triumvirate. This is an urgent, whispered exchange, in strong contrast to the revels around them, and it begs to be played downstage, with feasting continuing behind the conspiracy. It recalls Macbeth's exchange with the murderers during the feast at which Banquo's ghost is guest. Pompey will not play the murderer, however, and is furious with Menas for not having killed the guests himself. Honour prevents Pompey's involvement in such a crime, and the actor playing him has more evidence here of an exceptionally calculating and amoral figure. Menas's declaration to the audience that he will now abandon his General is the first of several betrayals by men of their masters in the play.

78–118   Menas's friendliness towards Enobarbus as the feast now continues is coloured by the former's plans to betray the triumvirate. The drunken energy of the feast intensifies as it 'ripens towards' the Egyptian-style revels that Pompey cannot help but mention again in

Antony's presence, and Caesar begins to express his distaste for the whole event more strongly. It is not necessary, as some productions have done, to portray Caesar as entirely self-controlled and coldly sober here, however. His comments at lines 93–5 can be played as expressions of regret that he has let himself 'wash his brain' rather than a refusal to join in from the outset; he certainly appears to be admitting having imbibed somewhat at lines 117–18. It is clear from his goodnight speech, however, that he is unlikely to want to join in the song and dance Enobarbus organises, and the F1 stage direction is interesting here. If Enobarbus 'places them hand in hand' and includes Caesar in the circle, Caesar might be reluctantly pulled about by the dancers, then break the circle before the revellers can start another verse. F1 has the song here sung by a 'boy' at first, to whom the men must presumably listen in momentary silence. As David Lindley points out, there is the potential here for a moment – or at least a vision – of real camaraderie as Enobarbus joins the men to dance, the illusion of which is then broken by Caesar (Lindley, *Shakespeare and Music*).

119 to the end   The farewells at the end of the revels seem genial enough, as hands are shaken and Caesar, perhaps, needs Antony to steady him despite his disapproving tones. Pompey and Antony's goodbye briefly reminds us of their enmity, though the thought is swiftly expelled by Pompey's expression of friendship. Enobarbus is keen to continue with the revelling, and we are left in the uncomfortable position of knowing more than the usually worldly-wise soldier, as the ostensibly friendly Menas invites him back to continue a party that would, if Menas had had his way, have ended in death.

ACT III

Act III, scene i

Ventidius's victory in Parthia.

This scene has frequently been cut in modern productions. Cutting it not only means a lost opportunity to stress the contrast between the revelling generals of the galley party and their subordinates in the battlefield, but leaves an abrupt time change between Act II, scene vii, and Act III, scene ii. Most editors add other Roman officers and soldiers to F1's opening stage direction, to chime with Ventidius's last line.

1–4   F1 has Ventidius enter 'as it were in triumph, the dead body of Pacorus borne before him', and his first speech suggests that war brings a violent but measured justice: Ventidius has killed Pacorus in revenge for the death of his compatriot Marcus Crassus. The dead body might be borne with some ceremony (though see also lines 36–8), and the contrast with the previous scene be made in terms of drunken bodies and dead ones, the latter having the greater dignity. Modern productions, notably Peter Brook and Peter Zadek's, have chosen to make the scene bloody and chaotic, however. In both these productions, the contrast with the previous scene pointed to the decadence of those who plan wars and the violent reality of war itself.

5–27   Ventidius's lecture on the danger of achieving too much in battle indicates that comparing generals and soldiers at this point in the play is far from just a modern tendency. Though the length of the speech suggests that it is hardly to be delivered in the exhausted last moments of battle, it certainly reminds the audience that for the soldier, fighting is a job, and one that does not necessarily reward individual achievements fairly. At lines 16–17, Ventidius baldly states that the timeless reputation of the likes of Antony and Caesar rides on the backs of their officers. The impact of the Generals on the lives of their men is made brutally clear at lines 25–7 – Ventidius's performance in battle as good as ceases to exist if he offends Antony by achieving at the General's expense.

28 to the end   Ventidius's comrade in arms, Silius, is determined that Antony should know of Ventidius's deeds in battle, and the actor playing Ventidius must decide whether or not to let his voice carry a degree of irony when he refers to Antony's name as 'that magical word of war' (l. 32). The soldiers plan to follow their general to

Athens and line 37 is a reminder that they are still carrying a body. This, combined with Ventidius's exhortation to the other soldiers on stage, might be read as justification for making this more of a breathless post-battle scene than I have suggested here. They are going to have to struggle along as fast as the dead will let them.

Act III, scene ii

Octavia takes leave of her brother.

1–22   This scene begins, rather than ends, with gossip and social commentary from those further down the social and military scale from the protagonists. The Romans are off to Athens after their successful dealings with Pompey, and Agrippa and Enobarbus joke about the events of the galley feast. There is much banter at the expense of Lepidus and his drunken praise of the other triumvirs. It is an affectionate banter, and the actor playing Agrippa might perhaps play the short line 19 with a touch of guilt at having joined in the parody so roundly. The call 'to horse' (l. 21) prompts the two to say farewell, but the entrance of the triumvirate and Octavia interrupts them and they stay to comment further on the conversation that ensues. Lepidus says nothing during this scene, and the actor playing him must decide how far the hangover of Enobarbus's quip (l. 6) should inform his performance here.

23–37   Caesar is clearly sad to be parted from his sister and reluctant to leave her to Antony. Antony stops the other man's passage across the stage at line 23 and despite – perhaps because of – the bond that is now supposed to hold them together, distrust between the two men is once more in evidence. Though it is right to play Caesar as genuinely affectionate towards his sister here, Octavia's lack of agency is again underlined in Caesar's first words. The loving expression Caesar uses to describe her (l. 24) turns into advice that Antony should use *Caesar* well in taking care of her. Antony reads the rest of Caesar's speech as evidence of offensive distrust (ll. 32–3) but it need not necessarily be played so. Caesar has good reason to fear that Antony will betray his sister, but here couches his advice in terms that implicate both men's responsibility in caring for her (ll. 28–33). Caesar is at least trying to be tactful in expressing his fears. Antony seems nettled, however, and protests rather too much in his own defence (ll. 33–8). The actress playing that 'piece of virtue' standing between the two men must decide how to react to her awkward position: How far has the notoriety of Antony and Cleopatra been kept from her? How far does she trust in Antony's fidelity?

38–50   Whatever the actress's decision, Octavia is clearly distressed at parting from her brother, and most modern editors add a stage direction that she should weep, to fit with Antony's comments at lines 43–4. This can be read as an awkward moment for Antony, who seems determined to interpret her tears and intimate whispering with her brother to his own advantage (ll. 43–4) or at least as a wavering between her love of the two men (ll. 46–50). It is significant that he describes Octavia in these speeches rather than addressing her directly. The only words he speaks to her when faced with her tears are a rather perfunctory 'Be cheerful,' denoting embarrassment at the display of emotion by a woman to whom he is married, but whom he does not really know.

51–60   Enobarbus and Agrippa now have a series of asides on the subject of masculine tears, as Caesar appears on the verge of them. Enobarbus is sharp and ironic on the subject, recalling Antony's tears over his rival Brutus. The soldier's admission that he caught Antony weeping seems a sarcastic one, but also reminds us of his closeness to Antony and the affectionate but exasperated feelings he seems to have for the General. The actor playing Enobarbus may interpret this as the first indication that he is to desert Antony.

60 to the end   As Antony and Octavia eventually leave Caesar, Antony affects a bluff cheeriness, perhaps to cover for the embarrassment at yet more evidence of his new wife's sorrow. His desire to show friendliness towards Caesar should be played sincerely enough here, but even this cheerful parting, in its language, foreshadows the conflict between the two men (ll. 62–3).

Act III, scene iii

Cleopatra quizzes the messenger about Octavia.

1–6   This next Egyptian scene follows closely in time from Act II, scene v; the messenger is cowering off or nearly off stage after Cleopatra's previous onslaught. Cleopatra has calmed herself and does not acknowledge that her behaviour might have terrified the man. She is clearly still distraught at her new loss but is now able to contain her fury and misery to hear what the messenger has to say about Antony's new wife.

6–25   Cleopatra's determination to interpret anything the messenger tells her to Octavia's disadvantage makes this a comic exchange. The biggest laugh must surely come at the queen's translation of the neutral report on Octavia's voice and stature into 'dull of tongue and dwarfish' (l. 16). The actress playing Cleopatra might acknowledge the audience here, either inviting their complicity or defying them to laugh.

The messenger's answers to the queen's questions are at first understandably short, and can be played as hesitant attempts not to bring on any further blows. He warms to his theme once he sees that she is now in the mood to be humoured, however, and his description of Octavia's creeping gate makes even Cleopatra balk a little at first (ll. 18–21). Her determination to believe what is clearly exaggerated or invented for her benefit thus seems all the more comical.

26–36   Most recent productions have played Cleopatra's reaction to the messenger's next pieces of information for its comedy value. The messenger can deliver the news that Antony's wife is thirty with a relish that suggests he believes this is ancient indeed, but gets a stony-faced reaction from most Cleopatras, as the queen is clearly older. He is on safer ground with the shape of Octavia's head and the colour of her hair; some productions have had Cleopatra's attendants help the messenger here by signalling to him the answers the queen wants to hear. Cleopatra swiftly regains her equanimity and gives him gold. The understatement with which she describes her treatment of the messenger as she asks him not to be offended by her 'former sharpness' should amuse the audience, as should her fulsome praise now that he has said what she wants to hear.

37 to the end   Once the relieved messenger has left, the scene ends with an exchange between Cleopatra and Charmian that indicates the waiting woman's determination to keep her mistress in this better mood by flattering her and agreeing with her at every turn. The scene is brought to an appropriately comic conclusion if Charmian plays her lines as desirous that this trying sequence would end. If the two women begin to exit during the exchange, Cleopatra might stop at line 44 as if about to call the messenger back, and Charmian can show palpable relief as the queen decides against it and convinces herself that 'all may be well enough'.

Act III, scene iv

Antony and Octavia speak of the quarrel between Antony and Caesar.

1–19   The scene opens in the middle of what is clearly an animated exchange between Antony and his new wife. Though she later describes herself as 'most weak, most weak' (l. 29) and, as we have seen, has little power to act on her own behalf, Antony's opening 'Nay, nay, Octavia' may suggest that she has been defending her brother with some degree of forcefulness.

Antony's honour and reputation are at the centre of his anger at Caesar here. Caesar has fought Pompey, against the terms of the treaty the triumvirate made with him (l. 4), but it is Caesar's reported reluctance to give him due praise in public that has truly enraged the General (ll. 4–9). Octavia is distressed at this revelation of what her position between the two men in their last scene together has come to mean. It is interesting that she is at her most forceful where she speaks of the conflict between the two roles – sister and wife – that render her most passive (ll. 10–19). She is articulate in her distress, giving expression to this contradiction with a bitter irony.

19 to the end   Antony's appellation 'Gentle Octavia' need not suggest that Octavia's lines have been spoken gently, and may contain some surprise at her forcefulness. His response centres again on his own honour, and contradicts somewhat his instructions to his wife in the last speech of the scene. What is odd about lines 20–4 is their suggestion that Octavia might well be better off returning to her brother given Antony's loss of honour at Caesar's hands. The actor playing Antony might read a lack of commitment to the marriage here.

Though she has not succeeded in making Antony forgive her brother or disbelieve the accounts of his disparaging speeches, Octavia does get her own way here to some extent and ends the scene with Antony's permission to act as go-between. Relief returns Octavia to the more conventional role of 'weak' vessel of Jove's power. She has one last, telling sentence about the cataclysmic consequences of a war between Caesar and Antony (ll. 30–2) before Antony closes the scene with what can be read as another oddly ambivalent exhortation to Octavia (ll. 33–6). He is clearly saying that one of the men is wrong in starting the quarrel, and ostensibly believes this is Caesar. The lines are not explicit in this respect, however, and once again the actor might interpret them as at least an unconscious element of self-accusation, or desire that Octavia return to her brother.

It is worth noting that Antony gives his wife freedom of choice as to how, and how expensively, she travels (ll. 36–8), to which compare Caesar's accusations in Act III, scene vi.

Act III, scene v

Enobarbus and Eros discuss the state of the triumvirate.

1–10   The two soldiers – the friend who is to desert Antony and the one who is to remain faithful to him to a violent end – discuss the state of the wars being waged by Caesar and Lepidus on Pompey, and Caesar's betrayal of Lepidus. Eros speaks what has been evident in the play to date – that Lepidus has been the 'poor third' in the triumvirate. Throughout this short scene, Enobarbus appears weary and cynical. Both men may enter at a similar pace, but Enobarbus's energy might drop when he hears the old news Eros has to offer (l. 5).

11 to the end   Enobarbus reacts to the tidings of Lepidus's capture with weary disgust at the world's doings. Eros's description of Antony's reaction is in marked contrast: Antony is clearly furious at both the killing of Pompey and the taking of Lepidus. The actor playing Eros must decide exactly how this anger of Antony's is to be physicalised as he imitates Antony on the word 'thus' (l. 14). However energetic a performance he gives, Enobarbus is not inspired by it. His response to Antony's summons brings this scene to a world-weary end (ll. 20–1).

Act III, scene vi

Octavia returns to Caesar.

1–19   This scene opens with another description of Cleopatra on display. This time, a furious Caesar gives the description, as he tells Maecenas and Agrippa of Antony's betrayal of Octavia. Antony has clearly not travelled to Athens, as Caesar later makes clear to his sister, but to Egypt where he has been establishing Cleopatra and her children as Queen of Egypt and surrounding lands. Caesar's words recall, but are in marked contrast to, Enobarbus's enthralled account of the barge trip down the Cydnus. Where Enobarbus immortalises Cleopatra with his words, Caesar is keen to show his contempt for the cheap public nature of Antony and Cleopatra's show (l. 11). There is no lavish description of Cleopatra's appearance here, though the audience will no doubt imagine that the event was similar in its extravagance to the one Enobarbus has described (l. 16).

20–39   The shocked Maecenas and Agrippa suggest delivering this news to the people of Rome, who will condemn Antony. Caesar has already been quick to do so. We then hear Caesar's version of the collapse of the triumvirate. Rather than describing Antony as angry at the renewal of the wars with Pompey *per se*, Caesar suggests that what the General really wants is his share of the loot. He does mention Antony's fury at the betrayal of Lepidus, but treats it rather dismissively with the word 'frets'. The audience might be temporarily confused at this, wondering just how faithful Caesar's account is, and whether Antony truly has self-interested motives for breaking with Caesar. Caesar's public condemnation of Antony before Maecenas (l. 23) might suggest an interested account on Caesar's part, however, and his description of the likeable go-between Lepidus as a cruel abuser of authority (ll. 33–4) makes him seem all the more calculating. In some productions this description of Lepidus has been treated as sarcasm on Caesar's part. At lines 35–6, Caesar clearly wishes to seem reasonable in his dealings with Antony, but lines 36–8 suggest that he has deliberately made Antony an offer he cannot accept.

40–61   Octavia enters, and some modern productions have had her enter alone. This makes Caesar's reaction to her greeting (l. 41) rather more sympathetic than if the F1 direction is obeyed and she is accompanied by some kind of 'train', albeit not a grand enough one for Caesar. For Antony truly to allow his wife to travel alone would have been extraordinary and Caesar's lengthy description of what her arrival should have looked like might then be motivated by astonishment. Her entrance with attendants will emphasise instead Caesar's desire for 'ostentation' for its own sake. Caesar is appalled at the lack of display provided for his sister's journey, and his lines on the importance of *showing* love (ll. 52–4) contrast with his disgust at display when Cleopatra organises it. In either case, the actor playing Caesar has to decide whether to embrace Octavia after what must surely be a hiatus between her greeting and his response. This would soften the lines that follow, which remind us of Octavia's primary role as peace-bond and status symbol in the Roman world. If Caesar remains at a distance from her, the lines may appear as much a rebuke of poor Octavia herself as of Antony, and lines 51–4 almost a threat from Caesar to withdraw his love. Octavia defends her husband by arguing that her mode of transport has been of her own choosing. It is ironic and yet moving to hear this woman talking of acting 'on [her] free will' (l. 58).

61–81   Caesar pulls no punches when it comes to disillusioning his sister about her husband's fidelity. His use of the words 'lust' and 'whore' indicate that his fury on his sister's (or his own) behalf may have blinded him to the sensitivities of that sister. Some productions have cut the list of kings that Antony has purportedly assembled against Caesar; the actor speaking the lines can offer them as Caesar's way of convincing Octavia as to the seriousness of her husband's machinations, or as an indication that Caesar is more concerned with the wider implications of Antony's betrayal than with Octavia's distress in the moment. In this section, Octavia does not indicate that she yet believes her brother regarding Antony's infidelity; at lines 79–81 she is mourning her impossible position, loving the two men as she does, rather than bewailing her abandonment.

81 to the end Caesar's next speech is calmer and more attentive to Octavia, perhaps as a result of the distress she exhibits at lines 79–81. His repeated welcome (ll. 81, 88, 93) suggests he knows that he has hardly been welcoming thus far. Agrippa and Maecenas offer their welcomes too, and Octavia might well break down entirely here. Maecenas is hardly tactful in returning to the subject of Antony's adultery; it is this last reference to it that really appears to wear down Octavia's resistance. Her forlorn question to her brother suggests she has no more arguments in Antony's defence. Caesar's last words are entirely focused on his sister, and his exhortation to patience (l. 102) might suggest she is weeping.

Act III, scene vii

Antony and Cleopatra prepare for a sea battle.

This scene marks the beginning of Antony's downfall as he heeds Cleopatra's advice before battle rather than that of his soldiers. It is a bustling scene of war-preparation, ending in a series of swift entrances and exits.

1–19 The scene opens in the middle of a lively argument between Cleopatra and Enobarbus as to whether Cleopatra should go into battle. The openness with which the soldier contradicts the queen is remarkable. She shifts from a furious, sulky familiarity in her first lines (ll. 1, 3–4) to an imperious royal 'we' at lines 5–6. Enobarbus is not a skilled manipulator and goes about attempting to win the argument the wrong way, first by making his dirty joke (ll. 5–8), presumably to the audience and given as an 'aside' by most modern editors. Whether or not Cleopatra half hears it, and her response (l. 8) is an expression of incredulity at his cheek, this is not the way to go about changing her mind. Nor is the argument that Antony's reputation in Rome is suffering (ll. 10–15). Where Roman honour depends upon reputation, Cleopatra's displays fly in the face of it. Although we might be inclined to regard Enobarbus as having a better understanding of battle tactics than the queen, her repost (ll. 15–19) is impressive, and might include the audience as an object of its imperious defiance.

19–53 Antony enters and immediately includes Cleopatra in his conversation with Canidius (l. 24). Antony enjoys Cleopatra's optimistic interpretation of Caesar's 'celerity' (l. 24). He is clearly in a mood for reckless heroism, and even an audience member who knows nothing of his fate will surely find his chivalric reasoning for fighting at sea (l. 29) an ominously thin one for going against the advice of Canidius, and then of Enobarbus – especially given Caesar's more pragmatic refusal of Antony's offers when they 'serve not for his vantage' (l. 33). The actor playing Antony must decide whether there is going to be a note of desperation amidst all this bombastic confidence or whether his enthusiasm for the sea battle is, in the moment, utterly sincere. He has no arguments to put to his soldiers, whilst Enobarbus's are watertight. At lines 39–40, Enobarbus's reasoning comes in short, measured sentences; however his speech of lines 41–8 is one long list of reasons that tumble out in just one sentence, indicating his desperation at his General's stubbornness. Antony's replies are short and obstinate: he might bluster about the stage waving his men away, or embrace Cleopatra as he attempts to ignore them. Cleopatra echoes his reckless delight in the idea of a sea battle with her offering of 'sixty sail' but says uncharacteristically little in this exchange overall. Delight at Antony's wild heroism presumably renders her admiringly silent. She might also throw some triumphant glances at Enobarbus or the audience, as if to point out how wrong he has been in his estimation of her influence. The exchange culminates in Antony's declaration that he will burn the ships he does not need and a casual plan to resort to land battle in the case of defeat. Enobarbus and Canidius no doubt look on, horrified.

53–66   A messenger's news of Caesar's victories and a desperate plea from a soldier that Antony should not ignore his wartime experience does nothing to dissuade Antony from his course. Again, he has no arguments to offer for his choice, and it is telling that he now leaves the stage, taking Cleopatra and Enobarbus with him and casually dismissing the soldier, perhaps before anyone can spoil his confident mood.

67 to the end   The fighting men left on stage seem all the more convincing in their belief that they are 'i'th' right' by virtue of the pragmatic nature of the ensuing dialogue. They express no relish in the glories of battle, but give simple news of the war and those involved. When a messenger calls Canidius to Antony, Canidius's closing lines might well be spoken with a desperate bewilderment at the way the action is progressing.

Act III, scenes viii and ix

There follow two tiny scenes, quickening the pace of the action as battle commences. Caesar and his lieutenant Taurus make their plans and exit; Antony enters with Enobarbus and puts the audience in the imagined position of observers of the routing that follows.

Act III, scene x

Antony's men mourn the flight of the Egyptian fleet.

Following the opening F1 stage direction here by having the two opposing land armies cross the stage would show the audience just how equal the two sides are, before Antony's sea retreat ruins his chances of success. The sea fight is 'heard' not seen, though; it is Enobarbus's reaction to seeing it that is the focus of the scene.

1–23   Enobarbus undoubtedly runs or staggers on stage here, and may cover his eyes as he recalls the sight that has 'blasted' them (l. 4). Scarus enters, presumably from the same direction, as he has witnessed the same sight as Enobarbus. Scarus's 'passion' (l. 5) is primarily against Cleopatra, and his are the most viciously misogynistic insults levelled at the queen in the play (ll. 10, 11). He tells Enobarbus what the soldier has not been able to watch – of Antony's flight after the queen. The violation of 'experience, manhood, honour' (ll. 22–3) this represents is ironic given the heroic optimism of Antony's decision to fight at sea in Act III, scene vii. One imagines two men wandering about the stage, unable to know where to place themselves to express their despair, or standing numb and bewildered – either way, a sorry contrast with the discipline of Canidius's army as it marches across the stage in accordance with the opening stage direction.

23 to the end   Canidius enters and his theme is a familiar one – under the influence of Cleopatra, Antony has not behaved like 'himself'. Canidius is going to desert Antony for Caesar, as many have done – but Enobarbus says that he will remain faithful to Antony. Modern editors have given the '*exeunt*' stage direction at the end of the scene, but Canidius might well leave first, leaving Enobarbus to speak his last lines wearily to the audience.

Act III, scene xi

Antony and Cleopatra reunite after the disastrous sea battle.

1–24   Antony here echoes the desperation of his men in the previous scene, in what must surely be a stagger onto the stage; his first two lines suggest that this stagger ends in a fall. Antony has entered with attendants before. Now he dismisses them, instructing them to take his riches and follow Caesar. It is as though he cannot bear anyone to be present in his moment of shame. The attendants are at a loss as to what to do – to obey their master is to abandon him. They do finally exit, though it is unclear whether they are going to take the treasure and leave for good as instructed, or not.

25–49   Cleopatra too seems to collapse almost the moment she enters (l. 27), surrounded by her own attendants begging her to approach and comfort Antony. Antony, it seems, cannot bear to see the woman he has followed to his disgrace. His repeated cries of 'no' and 'fie' seem to provoke further despairing reactions in Cleopatra – she might make to get up and leave, or sob uncontrollably at his reaction. Charmian and Iras are clearly reacting to some further show of emotion in their mistress at lines 32 and 33. Eros crosses to Antony, or else calls him to Cleopatra – he is clearly with Antony by line 51 – and is as concerned as the women that the two should comfort one another. It is a tableau of enfeebled masters and desperate servants. Antony now seems almost delirious in his misery as he remembers how much greater a fighter he was than Octavius Caesar in the triumvirate's quarrel with the murderers of Julius Caesar. It is unclear to whom 'my lord' (l. 35) refers, as Eros is hardly of a status to be thus addressed. At line 41, Cleopatra may try to push her women away, but then is persuaded to approach Antony (l. 44).

50 to the end   Cleopatra makes a rather feeble attempt to defer blame for the disaster when she tells Antony that she 'little thought' that he would follow her in her retreat. The exchange up to line 60 primarily comprises Antony blaming her for his shame and Cleopatra begging for forgiveness. The fact that Antony was so far in love with Cleopatra that he followed her to his doom appears to be her fault entirely. Once again, Antony falls in with the view of his compatriots, that Cleopatra enfeebles and emasculates him (ll. 64–7). Yet, interestingly, the actual presence of Cleopatra here appears to have a very different effect. Antony kisses her and seems instantly to revive and call for a feast. This might be played as a desperate or delirious bid to drown his sorrows, but I would argue that the audience should see a real and remarkable shift in mood here. Just as we have had it proved beyond doubt that Cleopatra is far from good for Antony, she re-inspires him.

Act III, scene xii

Caesar receives requests for lenience from the defeated Antony and Cleopatra.

1–25   That Antony has sent a mere schoolmaster as messenger to Caesar is proof of the downturn in his fortunes according to Dolabella (ll. 2–5). It is interesting that Dolabella finds it necessary to make this flattering argument to his master, though; it could be read as evidence that Caesar and his men are not entirely convinced that Antony has truly been defeated. On the other hand, the teacher/ambassador seems to confirm that his having been sent is a sign of Antony's newly diminished status (ll. 5–9). Caesar is suitably short and imperious with him, and the whole scene is a static and formal one. It suggests a simple tableau with Caesar at its centre, a contrast to the falling and weeping of Antony and Cleopatra in the previous scene. Caesar's reply to the couple's requests is certainly evidence that he should be played as a cold and calculating figure. He dismisses Antony's requests outright and offers to grant Cleopatra hers if she banish or murder her lover. However, one might motivate this cruelty with a mix of fury at the betrayal of Octavia or even, as we will see below, a fascination with Cleopatra herself.

26 to the end   Caesar's instructions to Thidias might suggest a more complex Caesar than the calculating authoritarian of some productions. One might read the flickering of a sexual interest in Cleopatra in his determination to bribe the queen into his power, particularly given the sexual connotations of perjuring 'the ne'er-touched vestal' (l. 31). On the other hand, Caesar might also speak the line with disgust. The actor seeking for an obsession with Antony will find it in lines 34–6, where Caesar demands a description of how Antony is taking his ill-fortune, prolonging the scene as Thidias is about to exit to do his master's will.

Act III, scene xiii

Thidias is interrupted by Antony.

1–12   Another scene opens with a conversation between Cleopatra and Enobarbus, one that again demonstrates a real familiarity between them. This time it is not an argument, however. Cleopatra plaintively asks who was at fault over the retreat at Actium, and it is as if she both wants and cannot bear to hear the answer Enobarbus gives. Enobarbus is a great deal more gallant in judging Cleopatra at Actium than Scarus was in Act III, scene x. He is absolutely clear that 'Antony only' was at fault (l. 3). Though this might be interpreted as another example of Enobarbus's simple, soldierly view of the world, I would argue that it indicates rather more of an ability to judge character than has been demonstrated by Antony's other compatriots. At least Enobarbus can conceive of both will and judgement in conflict within one man, and of that man having the responsibility to choose between the two. There is no talk here of Cleopatra's mysterious powers to unman Antony or transform him from his true self. What is striking about Enobarbus here, as in the first exchange of Act III, scene vii, is his ability to treat Cleopatra, too, as a human being like any other, despite the fact that he is as prone as the next man to awe at her grand displays.

12–28   Antony enters, in conversation with Caesar's ambassador, and expresses nothing but contempt at Caesar's offer to Cleopatra. Sniping at Caesar's youth, Antony proposes to dare him to single combat, so that Caesar might prove he is not simply a cowardly figure holding power as a child-king might do, through 'ministers'. Antony seems to have returned to the desperate heroics of the sea-battle plan here – he is playing out the myth of a gallant Antony rather than making practicable plans. Caesar has refused single combat with Antony before, but Antony has clearly forgotten this as he leaves with determined enthusiasm to write his challenge.

Cleopatra says significantly little during this exchange, and the actress playing her has to decide whether 'That head my lord?' (l. 19) is spoken in scorn at Caesar's offer, or whether the awkwardness of the phrase suggests a speedy consideration of her options under these new circumstances.

29–45   As Enobarbus says to the audience, it is ludicrous to think Caesar would give up his advantage by agreeing to Antony's challenge. Enobarbus's commentary on fortune and character here has an astute materialist ring to it. Now that Antony's circumstances appear to have lost him his judgement, Enobarbus begins to voice the possibility he might abandon his master. His second speech '*aside*' balances pragmatism with loyalty. For the moment, he still seems to favour the fame that loyalty against the odds might bring. Enobarbus's two speeches are inter-cut with Thidias's approach to Cleopatra, the casualness of which she interprets as in keeping with her reduced circumstances.

45–66 This is Cleopatra's first on-stage betrayal of Antony, if betrayal it truly is, and presents the actress with a dilemma similar to that facing the one who plays Cressida giving Troilus's pledge to Diomedes. Ought the queen to be played as utterly faithless to Antony, her 'O!' played as a keenness to grab at any straw offered her? Or should that 'O!' denote shock at Thidias's words, shock from which she must recover in order to pretend to concur with the messenger's suggestion whilst planning to betray or somehow escape Caesar later? Might she be delighted at the chance the messenger has offered to pretend to betray Antony but intend somehow to remain faithful to him? Though the modern actress may need to come to some decisions about motivation here, Cleopatra's actions and words in this scene will always be ambivalent. Enobarbus, however, reads no subtlety in her words, and the fact that even Cleopatra appears to be abandoning Antony seems to push Enobarbus closer to betraying him too.

66–87 Whether Cleopatra is merely playing at betrayal here or not, her flirtatious exchange with Thidias is an outrageous piece of over-acting and a performance she appears to relish. She answers pomp with pomp, responding to the notion of Caesar as 'universal landlord' (l. 73) with words that suggest abasement whilst still managing to be grandiose. Though not all modern editors give this as a stage direction, she could actually kiss Thidias's hand at line 76, supposedly because it stands in for Caesar's; she clearly allows Thidias to kiss hers, while reminding him of the great kisses that hand has received in the past. If this is a calculation on Cleopatra's part, Thidias appears to be taken in.

87–105 On re-entering with Enobarbus and finding a messenger taking liberties with his mistress, Antony is completely enraged. All he now wants is that Caesar's messenger should be hurt and utterly humiliated, because he reads his own hurt and humiliation into every circumstance in the scene. Even his servants' failure to appear the very second he calls for them is interpreted as authority melting from him (ll. 92–3). In a play preoccupied with whether Antony is 'himself' or not, this is surely the scene in which Antony is least like the Antony we have come to know and perhaps empathise with: here, ironically enough, where he shouts 'I am Antony still.'

106–34 Antony now throws every possible insult and provocation at Cleopatra. He begins with the legitimate children he might have had with Caesar's sister, and calling Octavia 'a gem of women' (l. 110) must elicit at least a wince from the queen. His next speech suggests that his eyes have now been opened to how love of Cleopatra has clouded his judgement. The queen can get only the shortest phrases in edgeways, as Antony goes on to rant about a sexual history that does not seem to have bothered him before, and to rail that she does not know the meaning of the word 'temperance'. This last might be regarded as somewhat hypocritical given the lack of temperance Antony himself demonstrates, and given his next speech, in which he figures himself as a savage animal roaring his outrage from the hill-tops.

The modern actor may want to motivate these speeches with more than the sight of a hand being kissed. He could decide that Enobarbus, off stage, has actually carried out his intention, expressed at lines 63–4, to ask Antony whether Cleopatra was truly forced into their relationship. As an alternative or addition, the actor might consider the humiliations Antony has already suffered at Caesar's hands and treat Thidias as a last straw – after all, Antony is clearly appalled at the low status of the man with whom the queen is flirting. These possibilities work better, I would argue, than having Cleopatra accept a blatantly erotic kiss. Whatever the actress's interpretation of Cleopatra, this scene is more engaging if her intentions remain ambivalent to the audience.

135–57 Antony's speech to the whipped Thidias surely contains his most unsympathetic lines in the play, and the speech has been cut in many productions. It begins with the ostensible reason for Thidias's violent punishment – the messenger is henceforth to associate ladies' hands with horrible pain; then Antony continues with what appears to be the real reasons for his wrath – his humiliation and helplessness at Caesar's treatment and his current fortunes. Antony's macabre offer of his own slave for whipping and torturing by Caesar seems to emerge from a desperate need to regain power over men's lives. Cleopatra's question (l. 157) indicates distaste and disapproval of Antony's actions, despite her own past treatment of messengers.

158–98 This section contains a remarkable shift in mood on Antony's part, as Cleopatra convinces him she is faithful to him still. If she is played as utterly sincere both here and in her previous reply to Caesar, the audience will be unsure which Cleopatra to believe. The list of punishments she calls down upon herself should she really have betrayed Antony (ll. 162–71) are all part of her self-mythologising performance throughout the play, but this does not mean they are not at the same time heart-felt. Cleopatra's character is produced in moments of conscious performance, so that we cannot dismiss her rhetoric here. It is also in keeping with Antony's self-dramatising moans at lines 157–8. Antony's questions at lines 160–2 indicate a gradual calming of his furious mood, and suggest that he moves towards the queen, more ready to be persuaded. But it seems to be her ability to paint an entirely 'Antony and Cleopatra'-centred world with her words that finally wins him round. A concern of the central characters in this play – Antony, Cleopatra, Caesar – is to immortalise themselves, and to control what is thought and said of them. When Cleopatra takes up Antony's rhetorical theme, his sense of self is restored. From the depths of despair he is optimistic once more; his description of himself in battle is of heroic arm-to-arm combat (ll. 182–6), after which he calls for feasting in the old Alexandrian fashion. Despair turns to a birthday celebration now that the couple have found themselves again (ll. 189–92) and though Antony's call to drunkenness may have a desperate ring to it – Enobarbus certainly thinks so – the audience might agree that this Antony is more Antony than the man who sent his slave off to torture.

199 to the end   If we are seduced at all by Antony's Dutch courage, Enobarbus brings us back down to earth in soliloquy here. This bravery is madness and will lead the General to his doom. For a scene that has just taken such an extraordinary upward turn, Enobarbus's final decision to leave Antony is an ominous ending.

ACT IV

Act IV, scene i

Caesar reads a challenge from Antony.

This short scene reminds us of the age difference between Antony and Caesar – and, at this point in the narrative, the difference in their mental states. Caesar reacts very coolly to the attempts at humiliation in Antony's letter. His response is dryly witty and he is in perfect control of his temper. He plans Antony's downfall swiftly and practically and has the resources and confidence to boost army morale by giving a feast. Maecenas refers to Antony as a dying beast, and we have just seen him behave in ways that make it an appropriate image. That behaviour is in strong contrast to the controlled coolness of Caesar here, whose last words, 'Poor Antony', can, on the open stage, usher in that 'poor' figure himself.

Act IV, scene ii

Antony says goodbye to his servants.

1–10   There is something of the bewildered child about the way in which Antony expresses his incredulity at Caesar's refusal to fight with him. He appears, here, to recover his mood through the rhetoric of blood and glory, but his farewell to his household servants will belie his bluster. Enobarbus humours Antony, but the soldier's promised battle cry will hold an irony for the audience, who know that he plans to leave Antony. 'Take all' might as well indicate surrender as victory.

10–34   Here, rather than angry or sulky at the turn in his fortunes, Antony is pitifully humble as he shakes the hand of each of his servants – a remarkable contrast to his fury in Act III, scene xiii, when the same servants failed to rush to his call, or the treatment of the unfortunate slave Hipparchus in the same scene. The exchange can either be played with a simple sincerity, or the actor playing Antony can add a note of hysteria to chime with Enobarbus's analysis at line 15. I would argue for the former; there is little self-aggrandising rhetoric here, though lines 21–3 are somewhat self-pitying. Enobarbus's alarm at this fatalistic farewell will be the more telling if there is no hint of a breakdown in Antony's tone. It is not only that the General cannot break down before his servants and soldiers in times of trouble; he cannot even speak simply and openly to them: his duty is always to appear invincible. The servants are clearly moved and bewildered by the exchange; this might be the first time Antony has ever shaken one of them by the hand, and a physical awkwardness between master and servants will make Antony's words seem all the more disconcerting.

Enobarbus and Cleopatra are once more very close here. Cleopatra seems either to defer to Enobarbus's greater knowledge of her lover when she asks the soldier to interpret Antony's words, or perhaps is disconcerted at encountering this new Antony, whose words and actions denote neither extreme self-confidence nor self-centred fury.

34 to the end   Though the exchange with the servants is obviously more sympathetic than his actions in Act III, scene xiii, it would be a mistake to interpret it as entirely altruistic on Antony's part. As Enobarbus points out, the General seems to be disregarding the distress he is causing them. But the fact that Enobarbus is on the verge of tears himself says something about the quality of Antony's speeches here. One somehow cannot imagine Enobarbus being provoked to weeping by an Antony wallowing in self-pity. Enobarbus's interjection brings about a sudden and contrived change of tone from Antony, who now tries to laugh off the moment and cheer the distressed servants. The fact that his closing speech is a call to drown sorrows in feasting suggests that this turn about is a forced one.

Act IV, scene iii

The watch hear mysterious music.

1–11   From the first line, this scene is thick with anticipation of the next day's battle. We never hear the 'rumour' the second soldier has heard, a fact that increases the tension of this opening. In contrast to Antony in his farewell to his servants, these men only want to encourage one another. However, though the bluntness of 'Here we' (l. 9) suggests a stoical reconciliation to whatever may come, lines 9–12 seem to betray something desperate in the soldiers' optimism. In the context of this dialogue, the F1 stage direction at line 8 conjures an image of men taking their positions in every corner of the stage, half-reluctantly, whilst determined not to show their reluctance. (See pp. 162–3 for Alan Dessen's reading of this stage direction.)

12 to the end   This moment is a potentially strange one for modern audiences, especially as there are no other physical manifestations of the mythic supernatural elsewhere in the play. The stage direction for hautboys under the stage indicates how the effect of ghostly music would have been created in early productions. The shortness of the lines here suggests a sense of hushed wonder amongst the soldiers, but the company might choose to speak with increasing dread and panic once the second soldier has given his doom-laden interpretation of the sounds, at lines 21–2. The repeated questions and 'how now's certainly suggest an increase in pace and energy from the quiet, tense opening of the scene.

Act IV, scene iv

Cleopatra helps to arm Antony.

1–18   Antony prepares once more for war, with Cleopatra playing a very different role from the one she took before Actium. Here she shows no appetite for fighting herself, and when she cannot persuade Antony back to bed, takes on the role of feminine helpmate as the General dresses for battle. Antony finds her endearingly incompetent as she buckles his armour. He expresses the wish that she could see him fight, but there is no sense in which this could really be a possibility. It is as if Actium never happened and Cleopatra has always been a gently teasing but ultimately submissive wife. Eros seems part of, rather than embarrassed by, the sleepy intimacy of the scene, staying to see Antony's dressing completed even after Antony has dismissed him (ll. 9–10).

19–34   The mood and pace change with the entrance of more of Antony's soldiers, and the F1 stage direction at line 23 fills the stage with shouting and trumpets. Antony's speech to the first soldier about rising early, and his next about the spirited morning, contrast with Cleopatra's sleepy fumbling, and she will seem an oddly feminine figure, presumably dressed for bed, amongst these armoured men. Antony repeatedly emphasises his masculinity in this scene. Calling Cleopatra 'dame' has the ring of a working man going off to his labours for the day. Even when he gives only a soldier's kiss, presumably less lingering than we have seen him deliver before, Antony seems to feel the need to excuse himself by explaining to his men how it would have been churlish to do otherwise. He then draws attention to the fact he is leaving Cleopatra behind, and to the image of steely masculinity in which he is constructing himself (ll. 32–3), indicating an awareness on his part of how he has recently failed to live up to the expectations of his gender and calling. With his last lines he establishes himself as leader in the ensuing battle, and he exits with his soldiers following.

34 to the end   The F1 text does not indicate where Charmian should enter, and most modern editors have her come on with the others at the beginning of the scene. It seems appropriate for Cleopatra to be the only female presence in the scene until the end, however, and there is no reason why Charmian should not appear just before she speaks her lines, as if she has seen Antony leave and thinks her mistress may want comforting. This is an unusual parting for Antony and Cleopatra; there is no tension or conflict around it, and no languid mourning on Cleopatra's part afterwards. Though the queen asks Charmian to lead her off, she seems determined to accept the gallant exit Antony has made, just stopping to wish Caesar had accepted his challenge, and expressing her doubts about the success of the day before accepting his departure with a 'Well, on.'

Act IV, scene v

Antony hears of Enobarbus's desertion.

The scene opens with Antony's admission that he was wrong to have insisted on a sea battle at Actium – but it can be played with a wry cheerfulness, to contrast with his tone when he hears of Enobarbus's departure for Caesar's camp. Even his general question about the deserters might have a bluff resignation about it. When the soldier names Enobarbus, however, Antony is reduced to a series of short questions that make it clear he cannot believe the news. His final call of 'Enobarbus' has been played both as a roar of pain and as an incredulous whisper. Either way, the moment is a potentially moving one. Antony's action in sending Enobarbus's treasure after him is certainly one of his most sympathetic.

Act IV, scene vi

Caesar makes battle plans; Enobarbus regrets his decision.

1–10   Having spoken a lofty three-line soliloquy on the universal peace he is hoping to create, Caesar is at his most cruelly calculating here as he plans to place Antony's deserters where the General can see them in battle. This will appear particularly savage to the audience, who have just seen Antony demoralised by the departure of Enobarbus. Enobarbus is on stage listening to this, and of course is one of the deserters to be thus used.

11 to the end   It is painful to see the bluff and humorous Enobarbus so far at odds with himself as he recalls the paltry rewards others have had for desertion; that the man who so relished the feasts and pageantry of Egypt should 'joy no more' seems almost impossible. To add to his pain comes the soldier with the news of Antony's magnanimity, which Enobarbus is now left alone on stage to contemplate.

His usual wry energy appears to have turned in on itself and his only wish is to die. The chosen place – 'some ditch' – makes the speech a radically different approach to disaster from the self-mythologising furies of Antony and Cleopatra.

Act IV, scene vii

Antony's victory.

This scene comprises two quick crossings of the stage. The wild energy of 'drums and trumpets', and Agrippa's desperate and Scarus's victorious cries, contrast with Enobarbus's weary exit in the last scene, and the audience will feel the irony of the fact that Enobarbus did not stay faithful to Antony for just a few days longer. As Scarus makes light of his scars, Antony's talk of blood and glory no longer seems mere desperate romance. It is as though Antony's men, even when wounded, are merely pausing for breath on their way across the stage to rout Caesar's forces further. The talk is all sport and sprightliness – a thoroughly upbeat scene for this momentary upturn in Antony's fortunes.

Act IV, scene viii

Antony meets Cleopatra after his victory.

1–11   This grateful speech from Antony to his followers is very different from IV.ii's pitiful goodbye to the servants. His first thought is of Cleopatra, but he appears to be entirely in control of his feelings and his war. He praises his men, calls them after a mythic hero and sends them off to bathe in the adoration of their loved-ones – but not before he has given instructions for the next morning's action (ll. 2–4).

11–27   Cleopatra has a different role to play for Antony from the wifely one she took on as he dressed for battle, but it is no less archetypally feminine. This time she is a muse of battle, the 'great fairy' who can bless the fighters' fortunes. The epithet 'day of the world' figures her as the fighter's glorious reward after the violent night of battle is over. It seems that she can inspire victory as long as she is not actually present on the battlefield. Antony's imagery is of himself chained and ridden upon by Cleopatra, but these read as words spoken in joyful jest. Many modern editors give an embrace as a stage direction after Antony calls her to him (middle of line 16). It would be quite logical to have the clinch come here, with Cleopatra's first words spoken in Antony's arms. An alternative would be for a hiatus here, a wondering pause in Cleopatra's move across the stage to the General as she expresses her delight at his miraculous return. In a gesture that is ironic given Antony's last reaction to his mistress being kissed, Antony now encourages Scarus to kiss Cleopatra's hand, as though it were a lucky charm. Cleopatra is more than happy to play the role of beneficent goddess, and she offers Scarus rich rewards.

28 to the end   Antony reclaims Cleopatra's hand, and his last speech whips up a frenzy of noisy triumph, building to a piece of typical Antonian rhetoric as 'heaven and earth' are called upon to join in the victory celebrations. Though I would argue that Antony himself should betray no desperation, but demonstrate utter self-belief here, those in the audience who know Antony's fate are unlikely to be carried along by the spirit of this speech. Yet another exhortation to drunken carousing before the next battle may sound warning notes even for those not familiar with the narrative.

Act IV, scene ix

The death of Enobarbus.

1–23   Another opening filled with anticipation of the forthcoming battle; this time it is the men of Caesar's watch who nervously await the early hours of the morning when they must engage again. They are interrupted by Enobarbus and witness what the soldier believes to be a completely private moment. In this extraordinary sequence, Enobarbus, it seems, commits suicide by willing himself to death. Though he has been a dry and sceptical commentator on the actions of his betters throughout the play, he has lived a life of soldierly loyalty; now he sees himself as a traitor and his life 'hang[s]' on him against his 'will' (l. 14). If the actor has succeeded in engaging the audience through Enobarbus's cheerful, cynical pragmatism, this exhortation to the moon and night to bear witness to his self-loathing and to draw life out of him will be distressing. He must choose whether to stagger and fall through the speeches of lines 7–23, or whether there should be something of a disturbingly deliberate ritual to his death. In many productions, Enobarbus makes no address or look to the audience here. This decision has a logic to it: he has withdrawn from us as he is withdrawing from life; he is entirely focused on willing his own life from him, and on the Antony he has betrayed. A last moment of contact with the audience would be poignant here, however.

24 to the end   The strangeness of this death is marked by the soldiers who witness it. The watch's approach to Enobarbus's body has a wariness about it; they do not know whether he is sleeping or has fainted, but their calling his speeches 'a bad prayer' suggests that they have been disturbed by his words. The second watchman's last line indicates they cannot quite believe he is dead. It is as though the death of this man 'of note' is as extraordinary to the common soldiers as it is to the audience. They take him up, and modern editors have added '*with the body*' to '*exeunt*' – and, indeed, '*He dies*' after Enobarbus's last words. In fact it remains uncertain whether it is a dead or dying Enobarbus that is carried off stage. The audience, too, will perhaps hope that 'he may recover yet'.

Act IV, scenes x and xi

Plans for battle.

A pair of short scenes in which F1 has Antony, then Caesar, march across the stage with their armies, planning battle strategy. Some modern productions have cut the scenes, or had only the speaking roles cross the stage.

Act IV, scene xii

The Egyptian forces fail Antony in battle.

The next day's battle is at hand and Antony is optimistic in the presence of the trusty Scarus. Once again the audience is prompted to imagine looking down upon fleets and soldiers making ready for the fight. Antony prepares to take up the best vantage point to watch the sea battle, with his foot soldiers at the ready. There is an unpleasant sense of *déjà vu* here, after Actium.

This sense of foreboding will be exacerbated by Caesar's words as he now crosses the stage; they imply a better understanding of Antony's plans than Antony has anticipated. The image of Caesar's army lurking in the vales whilst Antony remains looking out optimistically over his fleets from the hills is a sinister one.

1–9 Antony and Scarus re-enter and the atmosphere should be taut with the knowledge of which no one dares speak. Cleopatra's ships are not moving. Antony's first words should betray the desperation behind the superficial neutrality of his first speech, and Scarus darkly prepares the audience for the disaster that is to follow. This is the first the audience know of Cleopatra's involvement in the battle; we have last seen her waiting for Antony's return rather than witnessing the fight or planning battle strategy herself. Similarities with Actium will again be all too clear.

9–30 Antony's fury at Cleopatra's seeming second betrayal here may lead the audience to believe that it is she and Caesar who are celebrating Antony's defeat, where what Antony has actually seen – or imagines he has seen – is his men 'carous[ing]' with Caesar's. All we really know is that Cleopatra's fleet has engaged too late. The production company must decide whether this has been a planned betrayal or a fearful dithering on the part of Cleopatra – or indeed a betrayal by hesitation, as Cleopatra waits to see which of the men is likely to gain the advantage. For Antony, it is all too obvious. Cleopatra is both mystical nemesis – a 'grave charm' that has (mis)guided his every move – and a 'right gypsy', of whom he now attempts to speak with dismissive scorn. Antony seems as furious over Caesar's luck as with his own misfortune, but it is Cleopatra who is ultimately to blame: Antony's speech begins and ends with her. Ironically, Antony calls for 'Eros' – and Cleopatra enters.

30 to the end   Again, there is a decision to be made as to the deliberateness of Cleopatra's betrayal as she enters here. Is her question innocent or does it betray knowledge of exactly why Antony is 'enraged'? I would argue the solution is to play the line with absolute sincerity, leaving the audience in doubt as to whether this is Cleopatra the consummate actor, or whether Antony has simply misread her lack of action in the battle. Antony's furious dismissal of her prefigures the fate which Cleopatra finally kills herself to avoid: he wishes upon her the most humiliating of shows, a horrible opposite to the self-display for which she is so celebrated. When she has gone, Antony swears he will kill her, but the classical references he makes and the figuration of the queen as witch indicate that her execution is a violence that Antony has to mythologise in order to enact. He could, moreover, have run after Cleopatra and dragged her back, but instead calls for help from Eros. She is a 'spell', a 'witch' and a 'charm' in this scene, against whom Antony rails but who also seems to have rendered him powerless.

Act IV, scene xiii

Cleopatra plans her 'death'.

This is a race across the stage that takes up its energy from Antony's wrath in the preceding scene. The repeated call 'To th'monument' gives it a desperate momentum. It is almost as though Cleopatra has heard Antony's threats of Act IV, scene xii, though she left before he made them.

It is Charmian who first suggests that Cleopatra pretend she has killed herself as a result of losing Antony's love. It is Cleopatra, though, who dramatises it in her imagination and gives her eunuch instructions to describe her death for Antony's benefit. The rush towards the death of both protagonists, with all its unfortunate timings, has really begun.

Act IV, scene xiv

Antony attempts suicide.

1–22   Antony's opening exchange with Eros here is the logical conclusion to the lack of action that ends Act IV, scene xii, and the culmination of all the language of emasculation in the play. Antony now describes himself, to a seemingly bewildered Eros, as a cloud that momentarily appears as one shape before dissolving into indistinctness. He now not only blames Cleopatra for his downfall; he makes her the inspiration for all his actions so far, his reason for existence. Now she has supposedly betrayed him for Caesar, he describes himself as unable to 'hold' his own 'shape' – he has become 'not Antony' to the point of death, which he describes as the only possible action. He rather presumptuously includes Eros in this death wish, unless the 'us' of lines 21–2 is of the royal variety.

22–37   As Mardian enters – the man who has been robbed of his metaphorical sword – Antony declares that Cleopatra has robbed him of his. Mardian does what Cleopatra has required of him, dramatising the queen's pretended death and drawing out the description of her last words as instructed. The description is an ironically sexual one – Mardian might as well be describing an orgasm as a death; though Antony accuses Cleopatra of emasculating him, his name appears to have had an extraordinary sexual power at the moment of her death. The exchange between Mardian and Antony continues as sexual metaphor: at the climactic end of Mardian's speech, Antony lapses into an exhausted calm. Antony's dismissal of the eunuch is a potentially comic moment – it appears that Mardian is hoping for thanks or payment. This is one of several points towards the end of the play where the self-consciously high drama of the protagonists' deaths is juxtaposed and undercut with comedy.

37–55   Antony disarms, presumably with the help of Eros, to whom many editors give a stage direction here. The revelation of Antony from beneath the pieces of armour as they are taken from him, together with the sound of the 'bruised pieces' as they are discarded, will give a strong sense of something being dismantled – the soldierly Antony, as Antony himself describes it (l. 43). Instead of a miserable vulnerability, however, Antony expresses an absolute calm in his desire for death. Life and labour are pointless now that Cleopatra has supposedly gone, but there is ultimate fame in death to look forward to. Antony's image of the couple gambolling in the afterlife and stealing ghostly admirers from Dido and Aeneas might be conjured in a voice cracked with sobs, but might be more effectively and disturbingly delivered calmly. It is as if the pair can only live their mythic status in death.

Once again, the fact that Antony's attendant soldier shares a name with the god of love is used to ironic effect.

55–95 Even here, when Antony is describing his own dishonour in comparison with Cleopatra's supposed bravery, Antony draws upon imagery from the classics to elevate his drama to mythological heights. It is notable that he returns to the subject of Caesar; it is as much to escape disgrace at Caesar's hands (the disgrace he was wishing upon Cleopatra in IV.xii) that he plans his suicide, as it is to join his lover in Elysium. He now holds Eros to an old promise that the soldier would kill him rather than let him be disgraced – and it is clear from Antony's exhortation (l. 69) that Eros is horrified at the idea. It is a terrible, drawn-out exchange, in which Eros begs to be excused, then turns his sword upon himself.

This is not the noble Antony who insisted that Enobarbus's goods be returned to him. The sequence is, rather, comparable to the farewell to the servants; Antony does not seem to realise how cruel it is to suggest that if Eros does not perform this most seemingly disloyal of deeds, all his past loyalty will somehow be worthless (ll. 81–3). Antony appears too far absorbed in his own desire to meet Cleopatra in death to think of others that are dear to him.

95–104 The reading, above, of Antony as selfish in despair, is borne out by Antony's own condemnation of himself when he sees that Eros has killed himself. The words that he thinks are going to be his last are full of humility at what he knows Eros – and thinks Cleopatra – has done.

His attempted suicide now makes an ironic mockery of lines 50–4's lovely fantasy of death. The actor should not hope to avoid a laugh here as he exclaims 'How, not dead? Not dead?' The materiality of the violence of suicide attempted is absurd in comparison with the honour and glory of suicide imagined.

105–20   Again, the comic and the pitiful closely follow one another as Antony begs the guards who enter to finish what he has started. There is a horrible irony in the fact that they refuse; Antony calls for anyone that loves him to kill him – and nobody will. This does not suggest that no one loves Antony, so much as that the sight of the renowned war hero in his death throes is too much for any mere soldier to contemplate, let alone destroy. Antony is becoming both the myth of Antony and its opposite as he dies; the soldiers look on in awe at this 'star', whose fall indicates the end of time – and then they promptly leave him in a state of undignified agony. A last cruelty is shown him by Dercetus, who actually pulls out the sword from Antony's body in the hopes of using it to currying favour with Caesar. Dercetus will not stay to answer the questions of Diomedes, who now enters, and the Roman rushes off with his trophy.

120 to the end   The ultimate irony of the scene now becomes clear to Antony as he discovers from Diomedes that Cleopatra is alive. The dread that he is too late to save Antony will certainly colour Diomedes' speech. Antony, on the other hand, appears to remain calm in this new knowledge. Several actors have had him laugh at the ghastly irony that he has killed himself for nothing. He regains some dignity from the mess of the attempted suicide, as he requests that his guard welcome fate's blows rather than weep over him, and his last words in this scene are not agonised groans but thanks to his followers for their last service in carrying him to Cleopatra.

Act IV, scene xv

The death of Antony.

1–22   The actress playing Cleopatra must decide whether her opening lines are spoken with a terrible quiet assuredness, which unnerves Charmian into telling her mistress to 'be comforted', or whether her 'size of sorrow' is vocally and physically expressed from the outset. Many critics have complained about the drawn-out nature of the protagonists' deaths in this play. Beginning this scene at a high pitch of hysteria will give Cleopatra nowhere to reach for when Antony actually dies. There may be laughter through tears as Cleopatra calls upon the world to end when Antony does, as if Antony's end is simply impossible for her to take in. A genuine pleasure that Antony has conquered Antony might be mixed with the 'woe' that ''tis so'. The actress may decide that the queen can remain calmly certain of death until Antony's guard actually bring him into her sight; after that, her cries of help might mingle a bewildered weeping with the genuine need for aid in hauling him into the monument. Antony's statement that he himself, not Caesar, has triumphed here prefigures Cleopatra's own death. Antony refers to himself in the third person, as does Cleopatra, and the company must decide how far Antony's death throes are going to complement or contradict this grammatical aggrandisement. He immediately reverts to a simpler 'I am dying, Egypt, dying' at line 19, which might undercut the notion of a triumph over Caesar, or might lend Antony a quiet dignity.

22–41   The presence of Caesar still hovers around the scene, as Cleopatra foretells her own suicide and escape from Caesar's 'imperious show'. Her speech at lines 22–30 is almost a summary of Cleopatra's character: she is passionate, selfish, brave, preoccupied with show, jealous and humorous, all in these eight lines.

The scene has given rise to much scholarly debate around the practicalities of raising the dying Antony to the gallery of the Jacobean playhouse, and whether it was actually the gallery that was used for the last encounter between Antony and Cleopatra at all (see pp. 4–5). Whatever is decided upon in production today, I would argue that if the awkwardness of the lifting is 'solved' by modern technology, or by a simple staging that involves no lifting at all, part of this scene's meaning and emotional impact is lost. This is a moment where actual and fictional effort map onto one another in such a way as to both draw attention to the theatrical materiality of the moment and reinforce the emotional impact of the fiction.

Mimesis is in danger of failing in a moment of high emotion and Shakespeare acknowledges this; Cleopatra jokes about Antony's weight, allowing the audience to laugh at it too. The reality of physical effort will reinforce the performance of emotion as Cleopatra desperately kisses Antony once the lifting is over.

41–61   This last exchange between Antony and Cleopatra furthers the scene's extraordinary mix of the comic and the pitiful. The word 'heavy' shifts its meaning from the literal to the figurative at line 41, indicating that the scene is now going to proceed to the serious business of dying. However, when Antony calls for wine to aid his last words, Cleopatra interrupts him with her own determination to speak. Even when dying, Antony cannot get a word in edgeways, and Cleopatra reinforces the joke by recalling the railings of the nagging 'huswife', an insult she transfers from herself onto Fortune. The relative comedy or pathos of the scene will be affected by the position of the lovers here. If Cleopatra cradles Antony in her arms and, in contrast to the content of lines 45–7, speaks softly and ironically here, continuing to look at him, her attempts to defy Fortune will appear touchingly pathetic. If Antony has to draw her attention back to him from her railing, the scene produces a more comical but stronger Cleopatra. At line 47, Antony insists on speaking, but instead of moving straight to his own epitaph as noble conqueror of himself, he first deals with the practicalities of Cleopatra's life after his death, advising her as to who to trust of Caesar's men. The whole exchange gives the scene a precipitous rhythm, a sense of time running out before death. It also underlines the fact that Antony knows he is dying, whilst Cleopatra is determined to deny and defy his death to the last.

Antony asks Cleopatra not to think of his end as she remembers him, so much as of his former fame; for the audience, the sight of the self-wounded Antony may provide something of a contrast with his desired monumental image. The alliterative pomp of the epitaph he finally gives himself – 'a Roman by a Roman / Valiantly vanquished' – may do something to restore heroic dignity, depending to an extent on how much of a voice the actor decides to recover for this last moment. Certainly, after the gentle humour and thoughtful pragmatism of Antony in the dialogue that precedes his last speech, the audience may well be inclined to sympathise with this last moment of self-mythologising, or even to believe in it.

61–77　The moment of Antony's death comes during Cleopatra's next speech, many modern editors putting it at line 64 or 65. Though one should be wary about generalising over four hundred years about human reaction to death, perhaps this is a dramatic moment for which the historicist critic might risk a claim of universality. This speech – with its shift from incredulous questioning, to devastation, then emptiness – correlates remarkably with modern analyses of the process of bereavement. At the end of the speech, modern editors take Charmian and Iras's cries as an indication that Cleopatra is fainting, and this may well be her one genuine faint of the play. Charmian quietens Iras at line 77 as Cleopatra begins to recover and speak.

78 to the end　Cleopatra's comparison of herself to a mere milkmaid is a meditation on human frailty typical of the play's period – death reduces all to sameness, human power is nothing in the face of fate or the divine. Nevertheless, such tropes are dramatically engaging here, as they are so different from the ways in which Cleopatra claims power, visually and socially, throughout the rest of the play. The queen who has threatened to stab messengers and unpeople Egypt now identifies herself with those who do 'the meanest chares'. Now Cleopatra simply and logically makes clear her determination to commit suicide. Though she is intending to die 'after the high Roman fashion' there is nothing lofty in her language or her attention to her attendants. The simple rhyming couplet at the end of the speech echoes the brief resolution with which she now intends to treat her life.

F1 has Antony's body borne away here, and there has been some debate as to whether he should first be lowered again from the 'monument' to be borne by the soldiers who, it should be remembered, have been witnessing Antony and Cleopatra's last encounter. As Richard Madelaine points out, this may have been the original staging (*Shakespeare in Production*, p. 295). It would, of course, slow the action down at a point where many commentators have suggested

the play is too slow as it is. Lowering the body would allow for a ceremonious funeral procession of an exit for Antony, but if dignity was
the desired effect, this would be undermined by a repetition, albeit in
reverse, of the effortful hauling of the body. Most modern productions that have raised Antony on stage have had him removed from
his place of death.

ACT V

Act V, scene i

Caesar learns of Antony's death.

1–28   Caesar enters, with his council of war. His opening command
shows his frustration that Antony will not surrender, even in the face
of almost inevitable defeat. A brisk crossing of the stage is suggested
here, interrupted by Dercetus with Antony's bloodstained sword (ll.
24–5). To draw one's sword in the presence of the monarch was treason in medieval and Tudor England; even in modern production, the
bloody sword should be a startling sight. As Dercetus crosses the
stage to meet Caesar and his men, the momentary possibility of
violence breaks the mood of business-like irritation. Caesar's two
questions (ll. 4 and 5) might be used to suggest momentary fear on his
part, followed by a swift and imperious recovery.

Dercetus strikes a rather more honourable pose in this scene than
in Act IV, scene xiv, when he openly stated that he was taking
Antony's sword to Caesar in order to enter into Caesar's favours. It is
notable that whilst his first entrance is as an anonymous soldier – in
F1's IV.xiv he is not named – he now formally declares his name, links
it to Antony's, then offers his services to Caesar. His purpose is not so
much to deliver the news of Antony's death but to make a name for
himself. The dramatic gesture of offering his service or his life is lost
on Caesar, however, and the rhetoric that puts Dercetus centre stage is
deflated by Caesar's question at line 12. Caesar, it seems, cannot believe
he has heard Dercetus aright. Dercetus's announcement of Antony's
death, complete with the rhetorical flourish of an 'O Caesar', is also

met with a deflating reaction, as Caesar feels that something a great deal more momentous should have accompanied the news.

The actor playing Caesar will no doubt use this moment to inform Caesar's attitude to Antony throughout the play. Bevington draws attention to the fact that, whereas North's Plutarch has Caesar withdrawing to his tent for private grief, Shakespeare's Caesar 'use[s] the occasion for a display of his greatness', contrasting with the more intimate moment of Cleopatra's mourning. This reading, however, misses the opportunity for an emphasis on the awkwardness of public grief in a play so much concerned with display. Caesar can leave a stunned pause before his speech of lines 14–19 and speak with what is, in the moment, a genuine incredulity that the myth of Antony has not made itself felt in the world at his death. Dercetus speaks the rhetoric of the heroic Roman suicide in his following description, again, it seems, attempting to take centre stage and claim part of the moment's history for himself. Caesar's question to the 'friends' surrounding him, however, is strikingly simple and he is clearly crying at this point. Bevington grudgingly acknowledges that the tears appear to be genuine but adds that Caesar is 'not averse to having an audience' who can later testify to his humanity. It is, of course, possible for the actor to take up Bevington's through-line for Caesar and play him as almost entirely in control here, his eye constantly alert to the main chance of publicity. Without wishing to sentimentalise Caesar, however, I would argue that this is a moment of genuine vulnerability for the figure. He is confronted with Antony's death in a public, rhetorical fashion just as he is confronted with a bloody sword at the beginning of the scene, and the news, like the sword, throws him off his guard. The fact that he sees fit to justify his tears at lines 27–8 supports this reading. If the actor is permitted a moment of bewilderment here, moreover, the sense of this figure recovering command of himself at the end of the scene will be all the stronger.

28–48 The conversation between Maecenas and Agrippa seems a quiet, awkward one. They are discussing their own part in driving Antony to his death, and musing over his 'taints and honours' in a way that might be familiar to anyone faced with the death of a respected rival. Agrippa's comment that 'Caesar is touched', and

Maecenas's reply that Caesar will see himself in Antony, suggest that
Caesar has moved away from his counsellors to recover himself, a
reading supported by his longer, more controlled and declamatory
speech at line 35. In this speech he refigures his actions towards
Antony and his own tears as necessary, natural and dignified. There
is no reason why the actor should not continue to show emotion as
Caesar speaks warmly of Antony, but the 'Hear me good friends'
interrupted by the Egyptian's entrance at line 48 suggests that he has
recovered himself sufficiently to be aware, as Bevington suggests, of
the public impression of dignity and humanity his grief will give. He
has shifted from stunned incredulity, to distress, to funeral oration.

49 to the end   The Egyptian's entrance here must be an urgent one
to elicit this response from Caesar. This is the second time in this
scene Caesar has been interrupted with an abrupt and indecorous
entrance, and the pace of the scene again changes markedly. The
Egyptian is not recognised by Caesar as a messenger from the queen,
and calls himself 'poor'; his unremarkable appearance underlines
Cleopatra's changes in fortune. Now Caesar is to be given, he thinks,
the opportunity to keep Cleopatra in Rome, he takes another step
away from the momentary vulnerability of bereavement; his
language becomes formal, full of royal 'we's. It is clear that he intends
his treatment of Cleopatra to be a means of displaying both his
humanity and his triumph. His exhortation to Proculeius to hurry
lest Cleopatra commits suicide is an obvious suspense mechanism.
The last speech can be read by the actor as proceeding from guilt and
a resultant need for self-justification on the part of Caesar, as he
shows his friends how reluctantly he fell out with Antony. It can also
be interpreted as Caesar's expression of a desire to control, in every
detail, the figure he cuts in Antony's story.

Act V, scene ii

The death of Cleopatra.

1–36   As modern commentators point out, it is unlikely that this
scene of the play was played aloft in the balcony of the Jacobean

playhouse. The monument would simply have transferred to the main stage. F1 has Mardian enter here, but he says nothing throughout the scene; modern productions often cut him.

Cleopatra's opening speech seems to demand a calm and measured delivery as she gently scorns Caesar and earthly power. She is taking control of the 'accidents' of life by planning to end it, so it is appropriate that her speech should be controlled too. She plays remarkably high status in her response to Proculeius, treating her own position of weakness with a biting sarcasm. Considering this, Cleopatra's next answer to him is surely an exemplary piece of ironic theatricality on her part.

Proculeius's message from his master is overflowing with beneficence and the queen appears to respond to it as desired. Calling herself Caesar's 'fortune's vassal' indicates, however, a kneeling to the necessity of the moment only, a mere performance of obedience to the man she has just named 'fortune's knave'. The fact that Cleopatra is about to be taken by the Roman guard might suggest that Proculeius remains warily controlled in the face of Cleopatra's submission. Decisions here will affect how the entrance of the soldiers is staged. The movement of the soldiers into the monument has been staged quite literally in modern productions, with the men scaling parts of the set with rope ladders, for example; the capture will work just as well if the soldiers simply enter and take her, or if they enter with Proculeius and stand back from the action, waiting for their moment. If they enter from off stage or are somehow seen climbing into the monument, then the fictional timing of the capture is straightforward – the soldiers simply take Cleopatra when they reach her. If they are biding their time on stage, watching the encounter between the queen and Proculeius, then the moment of capture might come at a signal from Proculeius himself, indicating that Caesar's emissary is far from seduced by Cleopatra's performance.

36–63   The queen's capture precipitates an instant change of pace and mood, from gracious ceremony to a flurry of action. It is clear from Proculeius's words that Cleopatra now attempts her own life rather than be taken; she draws a dagger as modern editors have indicated. Proculeius responds with words that could not be less likely to persuade her to stay alive, begging her to 'let the world see' Caesar's goodness to her. It is precisely display before the world to the advantage of Caesar that Cleopatra is determined to avoid. Her first reaction to being thwarted in her effort to commit suicide is a furious despair that dogs, babes and beggars are taken by death and not she. Next she turns on Proculeius with her threats of suicide by starvation. The repetition of 'sir' in lines 49–51 suggests angry contempt for Caesar's emissary. Equal contempt is given Octavia; Cleopatra considers judgemental looks from one so 'sober' and 'dull' a fate worse than death: the queen would be subject to the gaze of her rival, on display in ways she could not control. Then, even at her most frustrated and miserable, Cleopatra has some extraordinary self-dramatising rhetoric. Her question followed by its three answers, each beginning with 'rather', is rhetorically structured as in an impassioned political speech. The imagery she uses to describe what she would 'rather' have happen to her than be displayed to the working classes of Rome is exceptionally ghastly, as Proculeius clearly feels when he describes her words as 'thoughts of horror'. Cleopatra has always been in complete control of displays of Cleopatra; rather than have Caesar take this control from her, she imagines a series of displays of herself in death that are as grim, but as visually striking, as the barge on the Cydnus was glorious.

63–93   Dolabella now takes over the guarding of Cleopatra and the queen loses her furious energy. Perhaps it is simply spent after the exertions of her last speech, and her message to Caesar at line 69 can be spoken with either a last burst of anger or a lapse into limp despair. Proculeius exits and many modern editors have the rest of the guard exit too. Emptying the stage of all but Cleopatra, Dolabella, Iras and Charmian creates quietness and intimacy for Cleopatra's 'dream of Antony' speeches. However, there is evidence that some guardsmen do remain (see Commentary on lines 93–109, below). If this is so, the actress playing Cleopatra will be responsible for creating the strange quiet of this scene. Cleopatra seems to speak with a soft-toned bewilderment (ll. 70–4); she does not appear to be building to a histrionic rapture on the theme of Antony for the benefit of a crowd, and rather than showing the absolute confidence of so much of the rest of the play, she is vaguely concerned that Dolabella will laugh at her. Dolabella attempts to interrupt her as she describes the Antony of her dreams, but she does not seem to hear him until his third interruption. Her thoughts of Antony here are not necessarily, of course, the literal description of a dream. They are an idealised recollection of the dead Antony. As she draws towards death herself, her speeches become dream-like and her imagery less concrete, more idealised. They are famously full of imagery of the spheres and the elements, creating a god-like Antony in the shifts from simile to metaphor.

The actress is likely to want to play these speeches with Cleopatra absorbed in the world of her dream, eyes glazed or staring away to the images of Antony she is conjuring for herself. Another powerful way of playing the sequence, though, is to have her address her speeches to the audience. There are different ways in which Cleopatra might offer to the auditorium this god-like version of the flawed man the audience have been watching. She might tell us her dream of Antony with absolute sincerity and as if 'Antony' is not a concept with which we will already be familiar. In this case, the effect will be of an almost delirious innocence. This reading would certainly add to the sense that Cleopatra is passing from this world and, she believes, into Antony's. Dolabella's interruptions would then denote a concerned calling of the queen back into the world of the fiction. She might also offer us the speeches in a rather more knowing tone, as if to say that no matter what we have seen of Antony, she wants us now to remember him in this newly idealised way. In this case, when she does finally pay attention to Dolabella, her question at line 92 might emphasise the 'you' of 'think you', sadly suggesting that she knows the audience might remain sceptical. After all, the notion that Antony's 'delights were dolphin like' – that his greatness somehow stood above the pleasures that preoccupied him – has not always been evident during the play. Either way, these speeches cast the audience in a very different role from that Cleopatra has offered them so far. We have, throughout the play, been her assumed admirers, occasionally thrown a defiant glance when our faithfulness has been in doubt. Here, Cleopatra can be seen to acknowledge us as part of a world outside her fiction – mysterious figures that just might understand Antony as she does.

93–109   Cleopatra's repost to Dolabella is a difficult one for a modern audience to grasp; its seemingly contorted figures of fancy and nature might pass for delirium on Cleopatra's part. The queen takes the argument that nature cannot compete with the imagination, and makes Antony her champion against it: to imagine Antony in the way she has done is to imagine what nature has truly created. Cleopatra uses the word 'shadows' to describe the workings of the imagination that do not live up to Antony's greatness; the word reinforces the idea that Cleopatra now regards this world as mere shadow and knows she is about to pass on to another. Dolabella interprets Cleopatra's discourse on Antony as the product of grief and offers her what reads as sincere sympathy. Cleopatra's questions to Dolabella before Caesar's entrance have a quiet pathos about them, and Dolabella seems compelled, against his desire to show Caesar as a worthy leader, to tell the truth about his master's plans for the queen.

109–35   Caesar and his train enter, and the meditative quiet of this sequence is instantly dispelled. 'All' shout 'Make way' for Caesar, and unless Caesar's followers are shouting at each other to make way, which seems unlikely, the exclamation would seem to contradict the notion that Cleopatra and Dolabella have been left alone: someone must remain in the monument for Caesar's followers to shout at. Having the shout coming from off stage can solve the problem, as if guards outside the monument are being moved aside, but F1 does give the entrance followed by the shout. If F1 is followed and there are guardsmen to move aside on Caesar's entrance, sense is made of what has often been seen as a cold disdain on Caesar's part as he asks 'Which is the queen of Egypt?' He asks the question as he glimpses three women through the group of guards through which he passes. On the other hand, on a large stage, with Cleopatra near the edge of it having just spoken to the audience, the convention whereby Caesar does not see Cleopatra properly until he comes nearer, guards or no guards, is easily accepted. This is supported if Dolabella rises and goes towards the direction of the shout of 'Make way there', has Caesar's question directed at him, then returns to the queen to explain who has arrived. Another alternative to the idea that Caesar intentionally belittles Cleopatra is that, on hearing she is to be paraded in triumph by Caesar, Cleopatra turns to the embrace of her women – or even the sympathetic Dolabella – so that Caesar cannot identify her. Dolabella might gently try to turn or raise her, but on hearing it is Caesar who has arrived, the queen kneels.

If it is the women who rush to comfort Cleopatra, rather than Cleopatra turning to them, the moment offers Cleopatra time to regain her equanimity in the face of Dolabella's confession, so that when she kneels to Caesar, she is back in control of her performance of submission. Certainly she seems to regain the ironic edge of her exchange with Proculeius in her dealings with Caesar here. Caesar asks her not to abase herself but to rise – and Cleopatra does so but marks the fact that she is obliged to do so because Caesar commands it. When Caesar, seemingly pleased with his own magnanimity, says that he will pass off as accidents her injuries to him, Cleopatra appears to offer complete submission to the 'sole sir o'th' world', but lines 120–1 suggest that Caesar is skilfully blowing his own trumpet rather than truly wishing her well.

Cleopatra's confession of women's frailty stands in ironic contrast to the images of suicide she has thrown at Proculeius and it will be clear to the audience that she has an interest in pretending frailty at this point. Caesar's next speech is one of his nastiest, beginning with imperial beneficence and shifting mid-line to the sinister warning of what will happen to Cleopatra's children if she should take her own life. The actress playing Cleopatra will no doubt wish to offer a reaction to this threat. The sycophancy with which she responds to a line of Caesar's that does not even require a response – 'I'll take my leave' – can certainly be read as a cover for a horrified reaction to the threat to her children. It is also in Cleopatra's interests, however, to keep Caesar on stage so that she can present to him the bogus account of the riches she has retained, which are the subject of the exchange that follows.

135–74 Editors, taking a hint from Plutarch (see p. 110), have read the sequence in which Cleopatra's treasurer betrays her to Caesar as a calculation on Cleopatra's part: holding back treasures will put Caesar off his guard, making him believe she wants to live, while she plans her suicide. However, it is difficult to see how this can be signalled in performance. Where modern productions have retained the sequence, Cleopatra has appeared genuinely furious with the treasurer. It is striking, on the other hand, that Cleopatra draws attention to her goods, unasked by Caesar. If the actress wants to motivate the showing of her accounts in a less complicated way than the aforementioned conspiracy with Seleucus, she might consider the explanation that Cleopatra is keeping back treasure for her children's inheritance and wishes to be seen voluntarily to be offering the accounts so that Caesar will not look into them further.

Cleopatra is as capable of acting in her own – or at least her family's – interests in this Act as in any other. Caesar tells Cleopatra not to blush, because he sees that she is genuinely mortified at having been caught out; her treatment of Seleucus is a repeat performance of her treatment of the messenger in Act II, scene v. Her fury is increased by the fact that, in the manner of a true aristocrat, she expects love and loyalty from those who have fundamentally materialistic reasons for serving her. Over two speeches she accuses the treasurer of a 'love that's hired' rather than sincere, but then names him as servant – a hired post, after all. Her fury also seems to claim a degree of class camaraderie with Caesar, despite the fact that she compares his 'lordliness' with her own meekness. The suggestion that they should change places (lines 150–1) in fortune, however hypothetical, seems to set them up as equals, and she calls upon Caesar three times in lines 149–74 to witness the faithlessness and ingratitude of servants. She speaks of the 'trifles' she holds back to greet friends with, as if Caesar will be familiar with such etiquette, and though she suggests that the women in Caesar's life are going to need inducements to be friendly to her, the picture she paints is of elegant aristocratic intentions thwarted by false followers.

Cleopatra's fury, just as in the messenger sequence, places her once more at the centre of the action. Caesar's 'Good queen let us entreat you' seems to be of no avail in calming her and his pose of imperious magnanimity can be undermined here, particularly if he is obliged to step between Cleopatra and Seleucus to protect the latter.

However, he could also signal that he finds the whole sequence hilarious, as Plutarch suggests (see p. 110).

The reference to Livia and Octavia is worth mentioning. Livia was Caesar's wife. The name will mean little to those who only know of Caesar through Shakespeare; those with a wider knowledge of the figure's history might be startled to be reminded here that Caesar has a wife at all. She certainly does not appear to figure in his thoughts or actions in Shakespeare's narrative.

Caesar dismisses Seleucus here, according to some modern editors, but his command that the treasurer 'forbear' does not necessarily mean the latter exits here. The word suggests that Caesar has some sympathy with the treasurer's plight and is asking him to tolerate Cleopatra for the moment.

175–89 Cleopatra continues either to figure herself as equal to Caesar, or to place herself above him if the 'we' of lines 175–6 is a royal one. The speech contains a distillation of the strange mix of performed humility and arrogant confidence that characterises the whole exchange with Caesar. She places herself with 'the greatest', then three lines later asks for his pity.

Caesar is now able to reclaim the role of benefactor, and proves as clever as Cleopatra at saying one thing and suggesting another. He tells her she may keep everything she owns, but in claiming to be 'no merchant' himself, might be having something of a dig at those who are mercenary. Then he tells her it is her own counsel that will guide his treatment of her, but ends line 186 with a command. 'Feed and sleep' may seem a kindly imperative, and should not be spoken with any sense of bullying. Yet however pleasantly spoken, it suggests that Caesar considers himself ruler over the very material of Cleopatra's life. Cleopatra now insists on returning to a ceremonious sycophancy and whether Caesar seems embarrassed by it or merely wearily amused will decide whether he has won this lengthy theatrical status battle.

190–206 Even if Caesar leaves the stage with his dignity intact, he is humorously undermined by Cleopatra in the presence of her women and the audience once he has gone. Her contemptuous use of 'words' as a verb shows that she has no time for his kindness. The conspiracy against Caesar's intentions is kept from the audience, as Charmian and Cleopatra whisper together about the plans for suicide. Iras's words at lines 192–3 are powerful in their simple figuring of life and death as light and dark. It is significant that a waiting woman from whom we have heard relatively little has more of a sense that this play is coming to its end than Caesar does. After this show of intimacy, Dolabella's betrayal of Caesar's intentions, as he tells the queen how long she has to carry out her plans, is moving. In a play that dwells often on friends' and followers' capacity for loyalty or betrayal, here is the queen at her lowest ebb, able to benefit no one, but nevertheless surrounded by people determined to act in her interests. Cleopatra, *pace* her lecture on the faithlessness of servants, does seem to be able to inspire a disinterested affection in these women and in Dolabella.

206–31   The lines in which Cleopatra imagines the show Caesar will make of her if he is allowed to parade her through Rome as his conquest, contain the famous meta-theatrical reference to the squeaking boy player who will play her in the humiliating pageant. Cleopatra may be painting this ghastly picture for her own sake, for Iras's or for both. The lady-in-waiting may need encouraging to take her own life, and the speeches persuade Iras that she should at least scratch her own eyes out before witnessing such a spectacle. Cleopatra may also be reminding herself of her own fate should she stay alive, in order to bring about the state of marble-constancy she will need to commit suicide. Whether or not the imagery here is a means of persuading herself to suicide, she certainly seems to become absorbed in her own revulsion at the imagined parade. What Cleopatra finds most horrifying is the notion of being displayed as opposed to self-display. Cleopatra controls the version of Cleopatra the world sees; Enobarbus's Cydnus description is eroticised, but nevertheless figures her as mythic, untouchable and in command. Here, Cleopatra imagines the working class taking control of the show, and she is lifted, caught at, breathed upon. The description is of a grotesque carnival that engulfs the Cleopatra myth with the coarse reality of stinking breath. Immediately juxtaposed with these images are her commands to the women to 'show' her 'like a queen'. It is significant that she recalls the Cydnus pageant at line 227. She is determined that the last Cleopatra to be displayed to the audience will be costumed and stage-managed on her own terms.

232–73   With very little foresight if he is one of Caesar's men, a guardsman lets the clown with his basket of figs into the monument. Having witnessed Dolabella's good offices towards Cleopatra, the audience might consider whether this guard, too, might be deliberately aiding Cleopatra's suicide. Cleopatra's speech on her 'resolution' to die reads as a controlled and deliberate preparation for death, a casting off of what we have seen of her character in the play to this point. A heroine more influenced by the 'fleeting moon' is difficult to imagine, and Cleopatra might address these lines defiantly to the audience.

Many modern productions have found it impossible to countenance any degree of clowning from the figure Shakespeare names as 'clown' here. Brook's 1978 production was criticised for its red-nosed asp-carrier, and alternatives have been found in the eerily innocent *idiot savant*, a sinister double with the Soothsayer and a doddering but serious old man. I would argue for playing him as a deadpan, pragmatic fool in the Feste vain, perfectly happy to make jokes and stray from his purpose at what are, for his social betters, the most serious and inopportune moments. His false exits, prompted by a clownish determination to stay on stage a while to make time-honoured misogynistic jokes, increase the suspense before the moment the audience knows is coming. The safety valve of laughter before the mimesis of death aids, I would argue, rather than distracts from the audience's engagement with the final moments of the play. Cleopatra seems only slightly frustrated at his refusal to leave, betrayed by the 'Ay, ay' before her second farewell, but her wry question at line 266 suggests that she is so calm in the face of death that she is happy to indulge him. If he takes centre stage and talks, as befits the clown figure, to the audience, Cleopatra seems resigned to being upstaged for a while as she knows her moment is coming. This reading is something of a compromise, perhaps, between one that insists on a serious clown so as not to intrude on Cleopatra's tragic dignity, and a reading that deliberately undermines this self-appointed icon before her death. I would argue that in order not to be merely irritated by Cleopatra, an audience needs to be seduced by her at some level, to lose its moral bearings as it tries to discern her intentions. When she dies, then, we are likely to feel both bereft of her presence and impressed by the last theatrical gesture of her suicide. Such an engagement will not be undermined by the interruption of a comic clown. Her interactions with him will remind us of what we have witnessed in Cleopatra throughout the play – a figure capable of utter disregard for those around her in one moment, and complete sympathy with them the next.

274–307   Cleopatra now hurries her women to dress her in her royal robes and the scene takes on a precipitous pace towards her death as she imagines first that she sees and hears Antony, and then that she is dissolving into fire and air. Her environment appears to take on the materiality of her wishes, as her kiss proves death to Iras. She reacts not in horror but with a kindly curiosity, and is convinced that death will hurt no more than a lover's pinch. Her calm will contrast disturbingly with Charmian's noisy distress. Even at this moment, Cleopatra seems capable of some mild humour, joking that Iras will reach Antony and kiss him before her.

The applications of the asp to Cleopatra's breast is a challenge for designer and actress alike. Imagined, property, and real snakes have been used. It seems unsatisfactory to render this most dramatic and self-dramatising of moments discreet and subtle by taking an imagined asp from basket to fabric-covered breast without the audience seeing it. Not seeing anything of the 'baby at [Cleopatra's] breast' smacks of a modern squeamishness about breasts and death. It seems much more like Cleopatra to expose the part of the breast she is coaxing the snake to bite. If the modern director fears sniggers at the wriggling of a real snake, Shakespeare has once again provided the emotional release of laughter within the scene, as Cleopatra scolds the 'poor venomous fool' for its lack of haste and wishes she could see it insult Caesar when he comes to claim her.

It is Charmian who reads the sequence as one of heartbreaking sadness, but Cleopatra is determined that her peaceful last moments should not be disturbed. Cleopatra dies, and Charmian is left to finish her last sentence for her.

The position in which the queen dies has given rise to some critical debate and a range of theatrical solutions. The stage productions discussed in Chapter 4 all leave her regally upright, and despite Caesar's command at line 350, which suggests that she dies on a bed, it is clear why. Dead on a throne or on some part of the monument that displays her in the robes she has chosen, Cleopatra leaves the audience, and Caesar, with a last image of self-created display – she becomes her own monument.

308–26   Charmian has a last, intimate moment with Cleopatra before Caesar's guard enter. Her words are a compelling mix of high rhetoric – she addresses Death and the sun god – and colloquial intimacy – she calls Cleopatra a 'lass unparalleled' and goes to straighten her crown before she is interrupted. She has now taken on the quiet calm of Cleopatra as the guard rush in on her, breaking the peace of the monument. She must either take another asp from the clown's fig basket, or take one from Cleopatra, though the latter decision might give away the source of death to the guards, who are later bewildered by it. Charmian is defiant in the face of the guard's anger and dies with as much quiet dignity as the queen. Her 'Ah soldier' mirrors her mistress's 'O Antony' and can suggest a last link between death and orgasmic pleasure. There may also be a sense of 'Ah soldier, if only you knew . . .' reminiscent of Hamlet's 'I could tell you . . .' (*Hamlet*, V.ii.331).

Dolabella enters, presumably pretending not to know what is likely now to have happened. His apostrophe to Caesar can be said with something of quiet satisfaction.

327–47   Once again, Caesar's presence is announced with calls for 'all' to make way, and once again a choice is to be made as to whether 'all' are the guard on stage, who step back from the bodies of the women, or Caesar's own train as they enter the monument. The echo of the previous entrance is ironic, as then Caesar came to the monument sure that Cleopatra was in his power; now he suspects what she has done. He admits defeat, though he might be reminding the assembled guard of how 'royal' Cleopatra was in order to present her death as a glorious inevitability, rather than a deed he might have prevented.

There follows an odd piece of detective work on the part of Caesar and his guard, which serves no purpose in the narrative, as the audience know how Cleopatra died. The sequence seems to work dramatically in two ways. It necessitates a decision on the part of the actor playing Caesar as to how near he comes to Cleopatra in death. Dolabella clearly comes close to her, as it is he who notes the 'vent of blood and something blown' that gives away the cause of death. Awed wonder or distaste at the sight of death might keep Caesar from the bodies, but wonder or prurience might as well bring him close. The fact that Caesar and his men remain mystified until line 345 gives Cleopatra power over her own spectacle even after death. The men have to gaze at that spectacle to read it, and indeed at lines 338–42, Caesar reads it just as Cleopatra would have wished. She looks noble, unspoiled by swelling, and as if Antony were in her arms.

347 to the end   Caesar's last speech is an attempt to reclaim a central part in the story of Antony and Cleopatra for himself. His statement that Cleopatra had been looking for 'easy ways to die' can be spoken either with humility – he should have guessed and therefore prevented the suicide – or with an air of knowing irony – she was always one to find the easy way out. His instructions for the joint burial are magnanimous, but his claim of 'glory' after Cleopatra has outwitted him seems to be making virtue out of necessity. I would argue that editors' attempts to make Caesar sympathetic in humility throughout the speech are implausible. Either the whole speech is an attempt to bolster his place in history after this historic failure to exert control over Cleopatra, or he has a moment of humility at lines 348–50, then spends the rest of the speech reclaiming his dignity.

In a modern production, Caesar's orders for a solemn funeral can signal a fade to black. Otherwise, the removal of Cleopatra's body on 'exeunt omnes' must be dealt with, and Caesar's instruction at line 350 gives rise to the aforementioned debate between bed and throne. If she is lifted on her throne, the last exit will provide an interesting echo of the triumphant parade Caesar hoped to make of Cleopatra.

3 The Play's Sources and Cultural Context

Shakespeare's primary source for the play is Plutarch's *Lives of the Noble Grecians and Romans*, written around the first century AD, translated into French by James Amyot and thence into English by Thomas North in 1579. There are passages in the play – Enobarbus's Cydnus speech for example – very close to Plutarch's 'Life of Marcus Antonius', and a selection of the more direct adaptations are included here. Shakespeare developed, from Plutarch, his explorations of 'the role of the great individual in the destiny of the state' and the 'problematic ideal of heroic selfhood', themes also to be found in two other plays with Plutarchian sources, *Julius Caesar* and *Coriolanus* (see Neill, *Antony and Cleopatra*, p. 7). Shakespeare also took selective inspiration from some of Plutarch's characterisation, and in other cases changed and adapted the ancient historian's figures and narrative radically. Plutarch's brave and morally upright Octavia, for example, is much reduced in Shakespeare (see below, pp. 107–8); Antony's magnanimity is the quality from Plutarch's history that Shakespeare emphasises over the cruelty to be found in the source.

Shakespeare may well also have read Mary Sidney's translation of Robert Garnier's *The Tragedy of Antony* (1595) and Samuel Daniel's *The Tragedy of Cleopatra* (1594) – though it seems that Daniel may in turn have been influenced by Shakespeare's version in his 'newly altered' edition of 1607. These Senecan dramas are written in strict accordance with the classical 'unity of action', and centre around the deaths of the central figures. They shed little light on Shakespeare's dramaturgy, but offer sympathetic portrayals of the pair to counterbalance some of the works more supportive of Caesar which were extant in English by Shakespeare's time. The historical Octavius

Caesar, it should be remembered, was regarded as having achieved his 'time of universal peace', and earned the epithet Augustus. His rule was considered highly significant not least because its period covered the time of the birth of Christ, and the Roman accounts of his story to which Shakespeare's contemporaries would have had access were highly critical of Cleopatra (see Hughes-Hallett, *Cleopatra*, pp. 36–69). However, as David Bevington remarks (*Antony and Cleopatra*, p. 6), even some of the accounts that broadly praise him also note his machiavellianism and cruelty.

Allusions to classical figures abound in *Antony and Cleopatra*, the pair being compared to Dido and Aeneas and to Venus and Mars; Cleopatra is referred to as Isis, Antony to Hercules, from whom he was legendarily descended. Bacchus, god of wine, becomes the musical centre of the galley feast. References to figures from the classics abounded in Elizabethan and Jacobean culture as a whole, and the sixteenth-century grammar school education that Shakespeare probably received in Stratford would have given him an early acquaintance with Latin literature, through which students were taught the rhetorical power of words. During the early seventeenth century a great number of Latin and Greek works became available in English translation. Thus the re-examination of ancient texts which characterised the Renaissance, and with it the ability to reflect upon the present using the ancients as metaphor, became an intellectual possibility for more than just the best educated in England. As we will see, even those of Shakespeare's audience without a basic education would have been familiar with a range of ancient historical and mythological figures through conduct books and playgoing.

The Aeneas of Virgil's *Aeneid*, Chaucer's *The Legend of Good Women* and *The House of Fame*, and Marlowe's play *Dido Queen of Carthage* provide, as Janet Adelman points out (*The Common Liar*, pp. 68–78), an anti-type for Shakespeare's Antony. Where Antony relinquishes power for love, Aeneas abandons love for politics, leaving Dido because he must marry politically and found Rome. Interestingly, Virgil's Dido is reunited in the afterlife not with Aeneas but with a former husband. When Antony makes reference to Dido and Aeneas losing admirers to himself and Cleopatra, then, he recasts the couple in a romantic ending that is in none of the Dido stories Shakespeare might have read. Here we can see not only the use of classical imagery in a Renaissance play, but more specifically its use by Shakespeare's Antony as he creates his own mythology around his love for Cleopatra.

On the Cydnus, Cleopatra displays herself as Venus, the goddess of love who captures the heart of warlike Mars. Later she dresses 'in th'habiliments of the goddess Isis' (III.vi.17), Egyptian goddess of fertility and the moon. Janet Adelman has pointed to the adulterous relationship of Venus and Mars as one of the 'ruling mythological commonplaces of the English Renaissance. Virtually any woman who managed to disarm any man could be seen as reenacting the victory of her divine prototype' (p. 83). Adelman goes on to discuss the different interpretations of the pair Shakespeare and his audiences had available to them, particularly through Ovid, who gives Mars and Venus the human qualities of adulterers finally caught out, and Lucretius, who represents their union as that between the cosmic forces of war and 'the great life principle of nature' (p. 84). Isis represents the exotic, alien nature of Egypt for Shakespeare's generation, who would have known her through Plutarch's 'Of Isis and Osiris' in the *Moralia*, translated by Philomen Holland in 1603 – but she also signifies fertility and regeneration.

Cleopatra, of course, hardly behaves in a particularly goddess-like fashion during the play. Shakespeare uses these figures not only to elevate his characters' mythic status but to reduce them to humbler humanity by comparison. The ancient gods themselves, in the sources whereby the English Renaissance knew them, were portrayed in lights both human and divine, both as moral figures and as representatives of cosmic forces.

Antony is compared to the classical demi-god Hercules throughout the play, and the historical Antony of whom Plutarch writes was legendarily descended from the figure. For the Jacobean London playgoer, Hercules would have been a familiar sight, supporting the world on the Globe theatre's flag, and years before that theatre was built, audiences could have seen Hercules portrayed on stage as a stock comic figure, 'a slow-witted creature of physical appetites and bombastic rhetoric' (Miola, *Shakespeare and Classical Tragedy*, p. 130). In the legend of Hercules and Omphale, Omphale dresses the hero in women's clothes. It is significant that when Cleopatra refers to him as a 'Herculean Roman' (I.iii.84), she has succeeded in making a ridiculous, ranting theatrical spectacle of Antony. Robert Miola has also argued, though, that Shakespeare's Antony appears in more serious, tragic vein; he, like the Hercules of Seneca's *Hercules Oetaeus*, 'experiences betrayal by a woman, rage, reconciliation, and (in some sense) transfiguration' (p. 141). Antony, like Hercules, is at once a soldierly hero and a self-indulgent fool.

The philosophy that Shakespeare and his contemporaries would most readily have associated with the Latin playwright and philosopher Seneca (4BC–AD65) was that of Stoicism; Seneca's works would have been readily available to Shakespeare in their original Latin and in translation, but even if Shakespeare never read Seneca's philosophical writings, they were the source of many Renaissance commonplaces about personal conduct. The good Roman Stoic eschewed indulgence in personal passions and achieved contentment in life through virtue, reason, calmness of mind and dedication to the wider social good. Suicide was not incompatible with Stoic values: Seneca wrote in one letter, 'Living is not the good, but living well. The wise man therefore lives as long as he should, not as long as he can – should my motto be "fortune is all powerful over the living", when it can be "fortune is powerless over one who knows how to die?"' (Seneca, p. 203). A man might end his life in accordance with Stoicism if he died in a state of calm and composure. These last are hardly the two words with which to describe Antony's life or suicide. However, that most unstoical, passion-bound of heroines, Cleopatra, dies in proper stoic fashion, calmly and with forethought, despising mortal fortune and extolling the virtues of constancy. Robert Miola suggests that Shakespeare might have found the Stoic Cleopatra of Act V in the *Odes* of the Latin poet Horace, who describes her as 'with face calm', 'resolved on death' (Miola, p. 187); in death she becomes the 'Stoic foil to her own fascinating changefulness, so achieving a paradoxical and moving combination of fleeting moon and marble constancy' (Miola, *Shakespeare and Classical Tragedy*, p. 189).

In this section, I have included a selection from Plutarch, Sidney and Daniel. As well as reprinting these direct and possible sources, though, I have suggested here the importance of what Janet Adelman calls 'the context of tradition to which Shakespeare could appeal in shaping his play and the attitudes of the audience towards it' (p. 53). A range of work on Shakespeare's use of Greek and Roman mythology and narrative can be found in the Further Reading section.

Plutarch's *Life of Marcus Antonius*

Page references for the Plutarch, Garnier and Daniel extracts are from Geoffrey Bullough (ed.), *Narrative and Dramatic Sources of Shakespeare*, vol. V; *The Roman Plays*, apart from the final Daniel extract (see p. 115). I have given modern spelling here, and retained North's punctuation except where use of the colon impedes the sense.

Antony's liberality – and flawed nature

But besides all this, that which most procured [Antony's] rising and his advancement, was his liberality, who gave all to the soldiers and kept nothing for himself: and when he was grown to great credit, then was his authority and power also very great, the which notwithstanding himself did overthrow by a thousand other faults he had.   (p. 257)

Cf. IV.v.10–13, in which Antony sends Enobarbus his treasure.

Antony's excesses

the noblemen . . . did not only mislike him, but also hate him for his naughty life: for they did abhor his banquets and drunken feasts he made at unseasonable times, and his extreme wasteful expenses on vain light huswives; and then in the day time he would sleep or walk out his drunkenness, thinking to wear away the fume of the abundance of wine which he had taken overnight. In his house they did nothing but feast, dance and mask. And himself passed away the time in hearing of foolish plays, or in marrying these players, tumblers, jesters, and such sort of people. As for proof hereof it is reported, at Hippias' marriage, one of his jesters, he drunk wine so lustily all night that the next morning when he came to plead before the people assembled in council . . . he being queasy-stomached with his surfeit he had taken, was compelled to lay all [i.e. to vomit everything] before them, and one of his friends held him his gown instead of a basin.   (p. 261)

Cf. II.ii.81–3, in which Antony gives a hangover as an excuse for his treatment of Caesar's messengers, and the galley feast of II.vii. This is also an interesting passage in terms of Antony's love of plays and performers and offers an Enobarbus-like example of long-suffering friendship in the friend who catches Antony's vomit.

Antony's resilience in adversity

Antonius, flying upon this overthrow, fell into great misery all at once; but the chiefest want of all . . . was famine. Howbeit he was of such a strong nature that by patience he would overcome any adversity. . . . And therefore it was a wonderful example to the soldiers, to see Antonius that was brought up in all fineness and superfluity, so easily to drink puddle water, and to eat wild fruits and roots. And moreover it is reported, that even as they passed the Alps, they did eat the barks of trees, and such beasts as never man tasted of their flesh before.   (p. 267)

Cf. Caesar's speech at I.iv.59–69.

Enobarbus

Domitius Enobarbus is very much Shakespeare's invention; he has only a minor role in Plutarch's history. In the play he is given something of Plutarch's own narrative voice – see, particularly, the barge on the Cydnus description below, and here where Plutarch's attitude to Fulvia's death is echoed in Enobarbus's blunt reaction to the news.

By [his friends] he was informed, that his wife Fulvia was the only cause of this war: who being of peevish, crooked, and troublesome nature, had purposely raised this uproar in Italy, in hope thereby to withdraw him from Cleopatra. But by good fortune, his wife Fulvia going to meet with Antonius, sickened by the way, and died in the city of Sicyon. (pp. 277–8)

Cf. I.ii.156; II.ii.101–5 and I.ii.114–17.

Enobarbus's death

Furthermore, [Antony] dealt very friendly and courteously with Domitius, and against Cleopatra's mind. For, he being sick of an ague when he went and took a little boat to go unto Caesar's camp, Antonius was very sorry for it, but yet he sent after him all his carriage, train, and men: and the same Domitius, as though he gave him to understand that he repented his open treason, he died immediately after.   (p. 298)

Cleopatra

Plutarch is ambivalent towards Cleopatra; at times he condemns her outright, and the motives of his queen are unambiguously self-interested in comparison with Shakespeare's heroine. However, there are also passages in which Plutarch appears to be as fascinated by her as is Shakespeare's Antony.

Cleopatra's negative influence over Antony

Antonius being thus inclined, the last and extremest mischief of all other (to wit, the love of Cleopatra) lighted on him, who did waken and stir up many vices yet hidden in him . . . and if any spark of goodness or hope of rising were left him, Cleopatra quenched it straight and made it worse than before.   (p. 273)

The barge on the Cydnus

The manner how he fell in love with her was this. Antonius, going to make war with the Parthians, sent to command Cleopatra to appear personally before him . . . to answer such accusations were laid against her. . . .

Cleopatra . . . guessing by the former access and credit she had with Julius Caesar, and Cneus Pompey . . . only for her beauty, she began to have good hope that she might more easily win Antonius. For Caesar and Pompey knew her when she was but a young thing, and knew not then what the world meant: but now she went to Antonius at the age when a woman's beauty is at the prime, and she also of best judgment. So she furnished herself with a world of gifts, store of gold and silver, and of riches and other sumptuous ornaments . . . But yet she carried nothing with her wherein she trusted more than in herself and in the charms and enchantment of her passing beauty and grace. Therefore when she was sent unto by divers letters ... she made so light of it, and mocked Antonius so much, that she disdained to set forward otherwise, but to take her barge in the river Cydnus, the poop whereof was of gold, the sails of purple, and the oars of silver, which kept stroke in rowing after the sound of the music of flutes, hautboys, citherns, viols, and such other instruments as they played upon in the barge. And now for the person of herself: she was laid under a pavilion of cloth of gold of tissue, apparelled like the goddess Venus commonly drawn in picture: and hard by her, on either hand of her, pretty fair boys apparelled as painters do set forth god Cupid, with little fans in their hands, with the which they fanned wind upon her. Her ladies and gentlewomen also, the fairest of them were apparelled like the nymphs Neriedes (which are the mermaids of the water) and like the Graces, some steering the helm, others tending the tackle and ropes of the barge, out of which there came a wonderful passing sweet savour of perfumes, that perfumed the wharf's side, pestered with the unnumerable multitudes of people. Some of them followed the barge all along the river's side; others also ran out of the city to see her coming in. So that in the end, there ran such multitudes of people one after the other to see her, that Antony was left post-alone in the market place, in his imperial seat to give audience: and there went a rumour in the people's mouths, that the goddess Venus was come to play with the god Bacchus, for the general good of all Asia. When Cleopatra landed, Antonius sent to invite her to supper to him. But she sent word again, he should do better rather to come and sup with her. Antonius therefore, to show himself courteous unto her at her arrival, was contented to obey her, and went to supper to her.   (pp. 273–4)

Cf. II.ii.200–28.

Cleopatra's relationship with Antony

Though Shakespeare's Cleopatra does not taunt him in quite the way Plutarch's does below, Shakespeare appears to have been inspired by the relationship described here, particularly in Act I, scene i.

The next night, Antonius feasting her, contended to pass her in magnificence and fineness: but she overcame him in both. So that he himself began to scorn the gross service out of his house, in respect of Cleopatra's sumptuousness and fineness. And when Cleopatra found Antonius' jests and slents to be but gross, and soldierlike, in plain manner, she gave him it finely, and without fear taunted him thoroughly.   (p. 275)

Plato writeth that there are four kinds of flattery; but Cleopatra divided it into many kinds. For she, were it in sport, or in matters of earnest, still devised sundry new delights to have Antonius at commandment, never leaving him night nor day, nor once letting him go out of her sight. For she would play at dice with him, drink with him, and hunt commonly with him, and also be with him when he went to any exercise or activity of body. And sometime also, when he would go up and down the city disguised like a slave in the night, and would peer into poor men's windows and their shops, and scold and brawl with them in the house, Cleopatra would be also in a chambermaid's array, and amble up and down the streets with him, so that oftentimes Antonius bare away both mocks and blows.   (p. 276)

See I.i.55–7.

The defeat at Actium

Now, as he was setting his men in order of battle, there was a captain, and a valiant man, that had served Antonius in many battles and conflicts and had all his body hacked and cut, who, as Antonius passed by him, cried out unto him and said:

O noble Emperor, how cometh it to pass that you trust to these vile brittle ships? What, do you mistrust these wounds of mine, and this sword? Let the Egyptians and Phoenecians fight by sea, and set us on the mainland, where we use to conquer, or to be slain on our feet.

Antonius passed by him, and said never a word, but only beckoned to him with his hand and head, as though he willed him to be of good courage, although indeed he had no great courage himself.   (p. 299)

Cf. III.vii.60–6.

Howbeit the battle was yet of even hand, and the victory doubtful, being indifferent to both; when suddenly they saw the three-score ships of Cleopatra busy about their yard-masts and hoisting sail to fly. So they fled through the midst of them that were in fight, for they had been placed behind the great ships, and did marvellously disorder the other ships. For the enemies themselves wondered much to see them sail in that sort with full sail towards Peloponnesus. There Antonius showed plainly, that he had not only lost the courage and heart of an Emperor, but also of a valiant man, and that he was not his own man (proving that true which an old man spoke in mirth, that the soul of a lover lived in another body, and not in his own). He was so carried away with the vain love of this woman, as if he had been glued unto her, and that she could not have removed without moving of him also. For when he saw Cleopatra's ship under sail, he forgot, forsook, and betrayed them that fought for him, and embarked upon a galley with five banks of oars, to follow her that was already begun to overthrow him, and would in the end be his utter destruction.   (p. 301)

Cf. III.x.

Cleopatra and Thideas

Plutarch suggests that Cleopatra might have been tempted by Thyreus, whom Shakespeare renames Thideas.

Therewithal [Caesar] sent Thyreus one of his men unto her, a very wise and discreet man, who bringing letters of credit from a young lord unto a noble lady, and that besides greatly liked her beauty, might easily by his eloquence have persuaded her. He was longer in talk with her than any man else was, and the Queen herself also did him great honour, insomuch as he made Antonius jealous of him. Whereupon Antonius caused him to be taken and well-favouredly whipped, and so sent him unto Caesar; and bade him tell him that he made him angry with him, because he showed himself proud and disdainful towards him, and now specially when he was easy to be angered, by reason of his present misery. 'To be short, if this mislike thee,' said he, 'thou has Hipparchus one of my enfranchised bondmen with thee: hang him if thou wilt, or whip him at thy pleasure, that we may cry quittance.' From thenceforth, Cleopatra to clear herself of all the suspicion he had of her, she made more of him than ever she did. For first of all, where she did solemnize the day of her birth very meanly and sparingly, fit for her present misfortune, she now in contrary manner did keep it with such solemnity, that she exceeded all measure of sumptuousness and magnificence, so that the guests that were bidden to the feasts and came poor, went away rich.   (pp. 306–7)

Cf. III.xiii.37ff.

Octavia

Plutarch's Octavia makes two journeys, one at her own request from Antony to Caesar, as in Shakespeare. Plutarch reports that she was 'great with child' by Antony at this time (p. 220), unlike Shakespeare, who suggests that their marriage is never consummated (III.xiii.108–10). Her second journey, to Antony while he is preparing for war against the Parthians, is included here because it reveals how Shakespeare has reduced the role of Octavia and made a more passive character of her. This passage is also interesting in the unambiguously selfish motivation it gives to Caesar.

> Now, whilst Antonius was busy in this preparation, Octavia his wife whom he had left at Rome, would needs take sea to come unto him. Her brother Octavius Caesar was willing unto it, not for his respect at all (as most authors do report) as for that he might have an honest colour to make war with Antonius if he did misuse her, and not esteem of her as she ought to be. But when she was come to Athens, she received letters from Antonius, willing her to stay there until his coming, and did advertise of his journey and determination. The which though it grieved her much, and that she knew it was but an excuse, yet by her letters to him of answer, she asked him whether he would have those things sent unto him which she had brought him, being great store of apparel for soldiers, a great number of horse, sum of money, and gifts, to bestow on his friends and captains he had about him; and besides all those, she had two thousand soldiers, chosen men, all well armed like unto the Praetors' bands. (p. 288)

> When Octavia was returned to Rome from Athens, Caesar commanded her to go out of Antonius' house and to dwell by herself, because he had abused her. Octavia answered him again that she would not forsake her husband's house, and that if he had no other occasion to make war with him, she prayed him then to take no thought for her. 'For,' said she, 'it were too shameful a thing, that two so famous captains should bring in civil wars among the Romans, the one for love of a woman and the other for jealousy betwixt one another.' Now, as she spake the word, so did she also perform the deed. For she kept still in Antonius' house, as if he had been there, and very honestly and honourably kept his children, not those only she had by him, but the other which her husband had by Fulvia. . . . Howbeit thereby, thinking no hurt, she did Antonius great

hurt. For her honest love and regard to her husband made every man hate
him, when they saw he did so unkindly use to so noble a lady.   (p. 290)

Cf. III.vi.40ff.

The death of Antony

Then she, being afraid of his fury, fled into the tomb which she had
caused to be made, and there locked the doors unto her, and shut all the
springs of the locks with great bolts, and in the meantime sent unto
Antonius to tell him that she was dead. Antonius, believing it, said unto
himself: 'What dost thou look for further, Antonius, sith spiteful fortune
hath taken from thee the only joy thou hadst, for whom thou yet
reservedst they life?' When he had said these words, he went into a chamber and unarmed himself: and being naked said thus: 'O Cleopatra, it
grieveth me not that I have lost thy company, for I will not be long from
thee: but I am sorry, that having been so great a captain and Emperor, I
am indeed condemned to be judged of less courage and noble mind than
a woman.' Now he had a man of his called Eros, whom he loved and
trusted much, and whom he long before caused to swear unto him, that
he should kill him when he did command him: and then he willed him to
keep his promise. His man drawing his sword, lift it up as though he had
meant to have stricken his master: but turning his head at one side, he
thrust his sword into himself, and fell down dead at his master's foot.
Then said Antonius, 'O noble Eros, I thank thee for this, and it is valiantly
done of thee, to show me what I should do to myself, which thou couldst
not do for me.' Therewithal he took his sword, and thrust it into his belly,
and so fell down upon a little bed. The wound he had killed him not
presently, for the blood stinted a little when he was laid; and when he
came somewhat to himself again, he prayed them that were about him to
dispatch him. But they all fled out of the chamber, and left him crying out
and tormenting himself; until at last there came a secretary unto him
called Diomedes, who was commanded to bring him into the tomb or
monument where Cleopatra was. When he heard that she was alive, he
very earnestly prayed his men to carry his body thither, and so he was
carried in his men's arms into the entry of the monument.
Notwithstanding, Cleopatra would not open the gates, but came to the
high windows, and cast out certain chains and ropes, in the which
Antonius was trussed; and Cleopatra her own self, with two women only
which she had suffered to come with her into these monuments, triced

Antonius up. They that were present to behold it, said they never saw so pitiful a sight. For, they plucked up poor Antonius all bloody as he was, and drawing on with pangs of death, who holding up his hands to Cleopatra, raised himself up as well as he could. It was a hard thing for these women to do, to lift him up: but Cleopatra stooping down with her head, putting to all her strength to her uttermost power, did lift him up with much ado and never let go her hold, with the help of the women beneath that bade her be of good courage, and were as sorry to see her labour go, as she herself. So when she had gotten him in after that sort, and laid him on a bed, she rent her garments upon him, clapping her breast, and scratching her face and stomach. Then she dried up his blood that had berayed his face, and called him her lord, her husband and Emperor, forgetting her own misery and calamity, for the pity and compassion she took of him. Antonius made her cease her lamenting, and called for wine, either because he was athirst or else for that he thought thereby to hasten his death. When he had drunk, he earnestly prayed her, and persuaded her, that she would seek to save her life, if she could possibly, without reproach and dishonour; and that chiefly she should trust Proculeius above any man else about Caesar. And as for himself, that she should not lament nor sorrow for the miserable change of his fortune at the end of his days: but rather that she should think of him the more fortunate, for the former triumphs and honours he had received, considering that while he lived he was the noblest and greatest prince of the world, and that now he was overcome, not cowardly, but valiantly, a Roman by another Roman.   (pp. 309–10)

Cf. IV.xiii; IV.xiv.22ff.

Caesar hears of Antony's death

. . . Caesar hearing these news, straight withdrew himself into a secret place of his tent, and there burst out with tears, lamenting his hard and miserable fortune, that had been his friend and brother-in-law, his equal in the Empire, and companion with him in sundry great exploits and battles. Then he called for all his friends, and showed them the letters Antonius had written to him, and his answers also sent him again, during their quarrel and strife; and how fiercely and proudly the other answered him to all just and reasonable matters he wrote unto him.   (p. 310)

Cf. V.i.12ff.

Cleopatra and Seleucus

When Caesar had made her lie down again, and sat by her bed's side, Cleopatra began to clear herself for that she had done, laying all to the fear she had of Antonius. Caesar, in contrary manner, reproved her in every point. Then she suddenly altered her speech, and prayed him to pardon her, as though she were afraid to die and desirous to live. At length, she gave him a brief and memorial of all the ready money and treasure she had. But by chance there stood Seleucus by, one of her treasurers, who to seem a good servant, came straight to Caesar to disprove Cleopatra, that she had not set in all, but kept many things back of purpose. Cleopatra was in such a rage with him, that she flew upon him, and took him by the hair of the head, and boxed him well-favouredly. Caesar fell a-laughing and parted the fray. . . .

Caesar was glad to hear her say [that she had reserved gifts for Octavia and Livia], persuading himself thereby that she had yet a desire to save her life. So he made her answer that he did not only give her that to dispose of at her pleasure which she had kept back, but further promised to use her more honourably and bountifully than she would think for. And so he took his leave of her, supposing he had deceived her, but indeed he was deceived himself.   (p. 314)

Cf. V.ii.119–89.

The death of Cleopatra

Now whilst she was at dinner there came a countryman, and brought her a basket. The soldiers that warded at the gates asked him straight what he had in his basket. He opened the basket and took out the leaves that covered the figs, and showed them that they were figs he brought. They all of them marvelled to see so goodly figs. The countryman laughed to hear them, and bade them take some if they would. They believed he told them truly, and so bade him carry them in. (p. 315)

Her death was very sudden. For those whom Caesar sent unto her ran thither in all haste possible, and found the soldiers standing at the gate, mistrusting nothing, nor understanding of her death. But when they had opened the doors they found Cleopatra stark dead, laid upon a bed of gold, attired and arrayed in her royal robes, and one of her two women, which was called Iras, dead at her feet; and her other woman called Charmion half dead, and trembling, trimming the diadem which Cleopatra wore on her head. One of the soldiers, seeing her, angrily said unto her:

'Is that well done, Charmion?' 'Very well,' said she again, 'and meet for a princess descending from the race of so many noble kings.' She said no more, but fell down hard by the bed. Some report that this aspic was brought unto her in the basket with figs, and that she had commanded them to hide it under the fig leaves, that, when she should think to take out the figs, the aspic should bite her before she should see her; howbeit, that when she would have taken away the leaves for the figs, she perceived it, and said: 'Art thou here then?'

And so, her arm being naked, she put it to the aspic to be bitten. Others say again, she kept it in a box, and that she did prick and thrust it with a spindle of gold, so that the aspic being angered withal, leapt out with great fury, and bit her in the arm. Howbeit few can tell the troth. For they report also that she had hidden poison in a hollow razor which she carried in the hair of her head. And yet there was no mark seen of her body, or any sign discerned that she was poisoned, neither also did they find this serpent in her tomb. But it was reported only, that there were seen certain fresh steps or tracks where it had gone. . . . Some say also that they found two little pretty bitings in her arm, scant to be discerned; the which it seemeth Caesar himself gave credit unto, because in his Triumph he carried Cleopatra's image, with an aspic biting of her arm. And thus goeth the report of her death. Now Caesar, though he was marvellous sorry for the death of Cleopatra, yet he wondered at her noble mind and courage, and therefore commanded she should be nobly buried and laid by Antonius; and willed also that her two women should have honourable burial.   (pp. 316–17)

Cf. V.ii.225ff.

Garnier's *The Tragedy of Antony*, trans. Mary Sidney

Cleopatra denies betraying Antony

CLEOPATRA

    That I have thee betrayed, dear Antony,
    My life, my soul, my sun? I had such thought?

> That I have betrayed my Lord, my King?
> That I would break my vowed thought to thee?
> Leave thee? Deceive thee? Yield thee to the rage
> Of mighty foe? I ever had that heart?
> Rather sharp lightning lighten on my head:
> Rather may I to deepest mischief fall:
> Rather the opened earth devour me:
> Rather fierce tigers feed them on my flesh:
> Rather, o rather let or Nilus send,
> To swallow me quick, some weeping Crocodile.
>
>   (Act II, ll. 387–8; pp. 368–9)

Cf. III.xiii.161–71.

Cleopatra can no longer weep over the body of Antony

CLEOPATRA

> Weep my companions, weep, and from your eyes
> Rain down on him of tears a brinish stream.
> Mine can no more, consumed by the coals
> Which from my breast, as from a furnace rise.
> Martyr your breasts with multiplied blows,
> With violent hands tear of your hanging hair,
> Outrage your face: alas why should we seek
> (Since now we die) our beauties more to keep?
>   I spent in tears, not able more to spend,
> But kiss him now, what rests me more to do?
> Then let me kiss you, you fair eyes, my light,
> Front seat of honour, face most fierce, most fair!
> O neck, O arms, O hands, O breast where death
> (O mischief) comes to choke up vital breath.
> A thousand kisses, thousand thousand more
> Let you my mouth for honours farewell give:
> That in this office weak my limbs may grow,
> Fainting on you and forth my soul may flow.
>
>   (Act V; 1983–2000; pp. 405–6)

Cf. V.ii.222–4; IV.xv.40–1, 71–6.

Daniel's *Tragedy of Cleopatra* (1599 edition)

Cleopatra determines to die rather than remain in Caesar's power

CLEOPATRA

> Of all, see what remains,
> This monument, two maids, and wretched I.
> And I, t'adorne their triumphs am reserv'd
> A captive, kept to honour others spoils,
> Whom Caesar labours so to have preserv'd,
> And seeks to entertain my life with wiles.
> But Caesar, it is more than thou canst do,
> Promise, flatter, threaten extremity,
> Employ thy wits and all thy force thereto,
> I have both hands, and will, and I can die.
>
> (I.i.45–54; p. 409)

Cf. IV.xv.51; V.ii.190–225.

Cleopatra on her waning beauty

CLEOPATRA

> And yet thou cam'st but in my beauty's wane,
> When new appearing wrinkles of declining
> Wrought with the hand of years, seem'd to detain
> My graces light, as now but dimly shining
> Even in the confines of mine age, when I
> Failing of what I was, and was but thus;
> When such as we do deem in jealousy
> That men love for themselves, and not for us,
> Then, and but thus, thou didst love most sincerely
> O Antony, that best deserv'st it better,
> This Autumn of my beauty bought so dearly,
> For which in more than death, I stand thy debtor,
> Which I will pay thee with so true a mind,
> (Casting up all these deep accounts of mine)
> That both our souls, and all the world shall find
> All reckonings clear'd, betwixt my love and thine.
>
> (I.i.171–86; p. 412)

Cf. I.v.30, 'wrinkled deep in time'; this whole passage dwells, as Shakespeare does not, on the notion of Cleopatra's debt to Antony, a debt she must pay with her own life.

Seleucus betrays Cleopatra

SELEUCUS　　Nay there's not all set down within that roll,
　　I know some things that she hath reserv'd apart.
CLEOPATRA　　What, vile ungrateful wretch, dar'st though control
　　Thy queen and sovereign, caitiff as though art.
CAESAR　　Hold, hold; a poor revenge can work so feeble hands.
CLEOPATRA　　Ah Caesar, what a great indignity
　　Is this, that here my vassal subject stands
　　T'accuse me to my Lord of treachery?
　　If I reserv'd some certain women's toys
　　Alas it was not for myself (God knows),
　　Poor miserable soul, that little joys
　　In trifling ornaments and outward shows.
　　But what I kept, I kept to make my way
　　Unto thy Livia and Octavia's grace,
　　That thereby in compassion moved, they
　　Might mediate thy favour in my case.
CAESAR　　Well, Cleoptra, fear not thou shalt find
　　What favour thou desir'st, or canst expect:
　　For Caesar never yet was found but kind
　　To such as yield, and can themselves subject.
　　And therefore give thou comfort to thy mind,
　　Relive thy soul thus overcharg'd with care.
　　How well I will entreat thee thou shalt find,
　　As soon as some affairs dispatched are.
CLEOPATRA　　Thanks thrice reknowned Caesar,
　　Poor Cleopatra rests thine own for ever.
　　　　　　　　　　　　　　　　(III.ii.671–696)

Cf. V.ii.140–89. Compare the reference to 'toys' and 'mediation' here with Shakespeare (V.ii.165, 169); Shakespeare did not find these in Plutarch.

Daniel's *Tragedy of Cleopatra* (1607 Revision)

The death of Antony

These lines, from a later version of Daniel's play, suggest that he may have seen a performance of Shakespeare's. Scholars have thus concluded that Shakespeare must have completed the play before Daniel's revision:

> . . . Which when his love
> His royal Cleopatra understood,
> She sends with speed his body to remove,
> The body of her love inbru'd with blood.
> Which brought into her tomb, (less that the press
> Which came with him, might violate her vow)
> She draws him up in rolls of taffaty
> T'a window at the top, which did allow
> A little light unto her monument.
> There Charmian and Iras, two weak maids
> Foretir'd with watching, and their mistress' care,
> Tug'd at the pulley, having n'other aids,
> And up they hoist the surrounding body there
> Of pale Antonius, show'ring out his blood.
>
> Gamini Salgado, *Eyewitnesses of Shakespeare: First-Hand Accounts of Performance, 1590–1890*, p. 27

4 Key Productions and Performances

Antony and Cleopatra has had an irregular performance history until the twentieth century. As we have seen in Chapter 1, little is known about performances in Shakespeare's time. The Restoration and eighteenth centuries were dominated by formal, heroic versions of the story, following the dramaturgical principles of Seneca and the dramatic unities. Dryden's *All for Love*, with its emphasis on love and honour, proved the most popular. Where Shakespeare's play was performed in the eighteenth and early nineteenth centuries, drastic cuts and transpositions were made to accommodate extravagant pictorial scenery, and collations of Dryden and Shakespeare were produced (see Bevington, pp. 47–51, Madelaine, pp. 26–74, Deats, pp. 37–8). Spectacular productions, with their concomitant reorganisations of the text, continued into the early twentieth century. Accounts of the play's performance history are full of entertaining details of extravagant processions and allegorical dances, enormous Sphinxes and working barges. The early twentieth century also saw, however, a revived interest in 'Elizabethan' production and Shakespeare's simple, fluid staging. Productions influenced by the 1920s' fascination for Egypt after discovery of Tutankhamen's tomb may still seem distractingly pictorial by today's standards, but a growing acceptance of an open stage as the best place to perform Shakespeare allowed for fuller productions of the Folio *Antony and Cleopatra* from this time onwards.

The four productions examined here have different relationships to stage space and audience, different principles underpinning casting decisions and the cutting of the text. The design aesthetic of each is different. However, each production has an open-staged sparseness in comparison with the extravagance of Victorian spectacle.

The first two productions, from 1953 and 1987, are dealt with together, as they were both large-scale productions in the mainstream, subsidised British theatre and both received praise for the simple drama produced by their sets and the engaging performances of the leads. I suggest, though, that their success was partly due to the ways in which they conformed to the conventions and expectations of the decade in which each was produced, and that in doing so, each production was able to smooth over some of the challenging awkwardness and tension that the 400-year-old text might have held for the twentieth-century audience. Some of the most interesting reactions to Glen Byam Shaw's 1953 production arise where the production *fails* to conform to critical expectation. The third and fourth productions assessed here are recent ones, and draw attention to themselves in terms of casting: the Globe's Cleopatra is played by a man, Manchester Royal Exchange's by a black woman, a significantly rare decision. Casting is not my primary focus however. I am particularly interested in these productions because they take place in theatres that draw such overt attention to themselves as performance spaces, and thus to the role the audience are given within the performance event.

Shakespeare Memorial Theatre, 1953; National Theatre, 1987

Glen Byam Shaw, 1953, Shakespeare Memorial Theatre.
Antony: Michael Redgrave; *Cleopatra*: Peggy Ashcroft.
Design: Motley.

Peter Hall, 1987, National Theatre.
Antony: Anthony Hopkins; *Cleopatra*: Judi Dench.
Design: Alison Chitty.

In April 1987, a number of enthusiastic reviews of Peter Hall's *Antony and Cleopatra* at the National Theatre compare it to Glen Byam Shaw's

1953 production at the Shakespeare Memorial Theatre, Stratford. Judi Dench and Anthony Hopkins 'rank with Ashcroft and Redgrave' in their 'comprehensive humanity' (*Guardian* 11 April 1987) according to Michael Billington; Charles Osbourne in the *Daily Telegraph* suggests that though the central performances, don't quite rise to the standard set by the 1953 pair, the production as a whole is even more successful than Byam Shaw's (11 April 1987). Tirzah Lowen's enthusiastic account of rehearsals and performances, in her book on Hall's production, mentions that Judi Dench and Peter Hall both consulted Ashcroft during rehearsal (Lowen, *Peter Hall Directs*, pp. 22–3).

Descriptions of the décor at the National echo 1953 Stratford too. Alison Chitty's curved wall and gateways with their 'broken surround and fragmented porticoes' (*Guardian*), breaking up and re-forming to suggest different locations, are more of a technical extravagance than design team Motley's shallow steps and cyclorama in 1953. However, both productions boast 'cinematic' sweeps from Egypt to Rome, a word first used in the 1953 reviews and much repeated in 1987, with rich, warm colours for Egypt and cold blues for Rome. Both productions have large casts, impressive period costumes – invoking the 'ancient' world in 1953, the late Renaissance in 1987 – plenty of brassy music for the battle scenes and a pair of star British actors as Antony and Cleopatra in each case. Madalaine remarks that the 1987 production 'seemed a little uninnovative' (*Shakespeare in Production*, p. 122), but there is something of nostalgia in the reviews for this lack of what is perceived to be a gimmick or 'affectation' (*Tribute*, 24 April 1987). The reviewers see in the National's *Antony and Cleopatra* a return to the virtues of a grand but not grandiose style, attention to verse-speaking, and fine acting capable of turning the most unlikely English actress into Cleopatra. Here is the ecstatic opening to John Peter's *Sunday Times* review (12 April 1987):

> Golden ages of the theatre are usually in the past – but we may be living in one today. Peter Hall's production of *Antony and Cleopatra* is the British theatre at its spellbinding and magnificent best. This is a big, heroic play in every sense. . . . Hall reminds us . . . that visual splendour and the excitement of action need to be justified by a sense that the words are both felt and understood. Without that we have theatricality, which is like inflation. Hall deals in sound currency. This is the real thing.

The rush of adjectives in the review – spellbinding, magnificent, big, heroic, complete, huge, great, symphonic, sensuous, burnished – could be from a description of Elizabeth Taylor's Hollywood entrance to Rome. Notwithstanding the fact that for Peter this is a British 'golden age', where splendour must be underpinned with a balance of feeling for and understanding of the text, Richard Elsom speaks of a 'sumptuous nostalgia for the grand style which gets in the way of making plain dramatic decisions' (*Critic's Forum*, BBC Radio 3, 18 April 1987). For David Bevington, however, it is as near a perfect modern production as is possible (Bevington, p. 70). He describes the balance achieved between 'disillusionment' and 'greatness', 'irony' and 'transcendence'. For both Bevington and Peter, the production seems to offer exactly what the theatre should in an advanced capitalist society: enough irony to give the thinking theatre-goer a critique of the heroic, but finally transcending its own particularities to reach a 'greatness' that is undefined, but both awesome and celebratory, something in praise of whose 'sound currency' the audience can unite. Though both productions demonstrate virtuoso theatrical ability, with lead actors who found a style of characterisation and delivery that epitomised good Shakespearean acting for reviewers of their time, I am interested in the ways in which each production smoothes over, or interestingly fails to smooth over, those elements of the play that 1953 and 1987 audiences might have found awkward or difficult.

In her account of women and representation in Shakespeare, Carol Chillington Rutter takes to task a long stage history of white Cleopatras, and argues that, historically and politically, 'blackness matters' in this play (Rutter, *Enter the Body*, p. 100). Rutter describes her shock at the 'embarrassingly crude' representation to be found in a photograph of Act III, scene xiii, in which two blacked-up figures – one rendered ludicrously shiny as the stage lighting bounces off her black grease-paint – are to be seen amongst the nervous courtiers who witness Cleopatra's encounter with Caesar's messenger in 1953 (p. 57). The 1987 production has had less time to become dated, and Alison Chitty's design neatly sidesteps choices and debates around race. 'The costumes', says the National's then resident designer when she meets the actors, 'will not be historical Egyptian or Roman but

Renaissance with suggestions of both, as in paintings of Mantegna, Veronese and Titian' (Lowen, p. 10). The poster for the production uses a Veronese image; the rich colours of the Egyptian costumes with their chiaroscuro glow, the darker ones for the 'classical/Renaissance fusion' in which the Romans are dressed, recall late Renaissance paintings rather than Jacobean theatre. 'All this not only places the action in the period when Shakespeare wrote the play; it also fits the mood and style of the writing', asserts the *Sunday Times* review (12 April 1987). It also conveniently avoids the now embarrassing theatricality of blacking up that would have been in evidence 'in the period when Shakespeare wrote the play', and, more pertinently in 1987, the decision as to whether to employ actors of colour. The production can thus concentrate on the supposedly universal human nature of the characters in this 'most human', according to Hall, of plays, rather than draw attention to the ways in which some cultures regard others as differently, or less than, human.

Byam Shaw's production took place in the year of Elizabeth II's coronation and around the twenty-first birthday of modern Shakespeare production at Stratford. It was a successful and, as Rutter argues, a conservative production by today's standards. However, I am interested in the critics' bewildered and contradictory responses to Ashcroft in the role of Cleopatra. They suggest that the 1953 production does not hold together in the ways for which Dench's performance is so roundly praised, and that it is possible to find productive cracks in its dominant theme of tragic character development against an exotic backdrop.

Tirzah Lowen's account of rehearsals and performances at the National paints a clear picture of the balance between psychological and technical approaches maintained by British actors approaching Shakespeare. On the one hand, Judi Dench's process appears intensely psychological. Like many actors talking about their characters, she speaks about Cleopatra as if she were a real person with a life outside of the play. Hall has to dampen her enthusiasm for research which reveals 'that when Antony returned to Rome', the historical Cleopatra 'was carrying twins, born just before his marriage to Octavia. She [Dench] felt it put everything into perspective.' Hall reminds Judi Dench that 'It's not in Shakespeare' (p. 53). On the other hand, Lowen describes Dench as having an affinity for Hall's approach to Shakespearean verse, an approach which stems from his awareness of verse as a rhetorical device in the open-air theatre. Hall insists on using the beat of the iambic pentameter rather than attempting to naturalise it. 'Keeping to the beat of the line makes it fleet: Hamlet's advice to the players, that the speech be spoken "trippingly on the tongue", is worth all of Stanislavski in doing Shakespeare' (p. 27). What emerges in reviews, and is certainly not something Hall would wish to avoid, is a strong sense of psychological character none the less. What impresses John Peter, and adds to rather than contradicts his sense of this production as heroic, complete, huge, great etc., is that

> Antony Hopkins and Judi Dench play the title roles as if they were not star actors. There is a moving and painful honesty in these performances: they are fleshy, aging people, both of them attractive and difficult, and they give out a sense of searing, wounded intimacy.

Several reviewers note the sense, created by the production, of an aging love coming to an end, and this 'menopausal love' is something Hall was keen to explore in rehearsal. Dench talks of 'Cleopatra's awareness that this is the last great passion of her life' (Lowen, p. 57). Irving Wardle's review in *The Times* sums up how realist characterisation works against décor to produce meaning here:

> The effect is to create an idealized environment. Costume and setting alike proclaim heroic perfection: absolute purity of love, invincible physical and moral strength. The opposite, in short, of the aging couple whose besotted love destroys them and their empires.   (*The Times*, 11 April 1987)

What emerges eventually in Wardle's review is an Antony and Cleopatra who do not so much fail to live up to their myth, but who go beyond it with something more 'human', and very distinctly gendered. Antony is 'a man with too much dignity to exhibit his real despair to his followers' (which is odd, given how explicitly Enobarbus shows that he has recognised this despair in Act IV, scene ii). Cleopatra, 'just when such a thing seems impossible . . . melts into submissiveness and the true voice of feeling'. With this degree of sentimental humanism to reassure reviewers such as Wardle, it is unsurprising that moments where Antony is less than dignified are not cut in this production, as they are in Byam Shaw's. The 'pettiest emotions' are played against the grandeur of the 'idealised environment', but they need not disturb our sense of the greatness of the human spirit. Indeed, the whims and tempers of the two main characters help to produce rather than puncture empathy with the pair. The lovers achieve greatness in dignified death both despite and because of their realist portrayal as middle-aged.

In 1953, Shakespearean tragedy clearly demanded something less 'menopausal', more archetypally and decorously heroic. Hopkins and Dench roll around on the floor together, in the sight of the disapproving messengers from Rome, signalling their at once selfish and warmly 'human' disregard for the roles and reputations they are to recover in death. Redgrave and Ashcroft make love less effusively. Amongst the photographs of the 1953 production are two images of a moment from Act I, scene i: a clinch, in which Antony and Cleopatra are linked with a voluptuous garland of leaves and flowers. Redgrave is kissing Ashcroft's cheek, one hand cradling her neck and head as he does so, the other on her upper arm to complete the embrace; his expression appears half way between pleading and smiling. Though Ashcroft is pulled close to him, her hand is placed against his chest, as if fending him off. She is looking away from him and her smile is tolerant, patronising, with perhaps a hint of discomfort to accompany that warning hand. It is as if Antony has misinterpreted the moment and forced an intimacy on Cleopatra that she refuses. Her servants look nervously on.

Reviewers of both these productions express surprise at the casting of Cleopatra in terms of perceived notions of sensuality and sexual attractiveness. Dench appears ultimately to cause less consternation for not being a young, darkly exotic siren than does Ashcroft, and I suggest that Dench is more readily accepted as Cleopatra because the National production erases problems around the figure's otherness; Judi Dench makes Cleopatra a recognisably naturalistic character. Ashcroft's restraining hand in the photograph could be read as part of that English *froideur* that, it seems, was expected of home-grown Cleopatras since Mrs Siddons said that 'she should hate herself if she played the part as it ought to be played' (quoted in the *News Chronicle* review of the 1953 production, 19 April 1953). As we will see, a range of reviewers read Ashcroft's Cleopatra as lacking in dangerous, exotic sensuality. However, the reviewer who quotes Siddons is impressed that Ashcroft's performance is as 'fundamentally sensual' as Siddons felt it should be: Ashcroft 'contrives to be all the things, both complimentary and abusive, that Cleopatra is called'. The reviewers who revive the debate about Englishness appear surprised, even disconcerted by the notion of a nicely spoken white woman playing this role; the production does not appear to have eradicated Cleopatra's threatening sensuality – or even, as we shall see, her racial otherness – by casting Peggy Ashcroft.

Another, wider, shot of the 1953 production, and one even fuller of attendants, is of Act IV, scene viii, Antony's meeting with Cleopatra after his triumphant return from battle. The shot is set up on the curved, shallow staircase that backs Motley's set. The attendants are ranged around the top of the staircase holding jewelled branches. Cleopatra descends the stairs to Antony, her head tilted and her arms outstretched in extravagant welcome; Antony's arms are stretched even wider. Of course, this is a posed photograph of what might, in production, have been a swift move into each other's arms. It is as easy to imagine, however, that this is a display of triumph and togetherness that takes place as a hiatus in the performance itself – a deliberate histrionic pause as Antony calls upon the 'day o'th' world' to 'chain [his] armed neck'. Interestingly, Lowen writes about a version of IV.viii in the Hall production which emerged in rehearsal and bore some similarity to the 1953 scene, but which was replaced by something less formal and more psychologically intricate as the production developed. Here Lowen describes the first version:

> For the triumphal return to Alexandria, [Antony] and his soldiers, accompanied by drum rolls, will come down the centre aisle of the theatre and up onto the stage, with the doors rolling back before them. . . . Cleopatra emerges, to be greeted by full bows of Elizabethan gallantry. . . . Peter Hall wants 'a sense of the miraculous' and urges space between her and Antony. The lyrical language is enormously moving as they face one another, first apart in wonderment, then moving in to embrace. (p. 39)

Later, Hall apparently

> decides to break away from formality in Act IV Scene 8, and have the
> small, unexpectedly victorious army come down the centre aisle in joyful
> disarray. He asks the actors to react freely; whooping and cheering they
> spread themselves across the stage . . .

He and Dench clearly want to avoid cliché here:

> Emerging, Dench conveys her wonder and disbelief at the triumph. (Hall:
> 'The problem with this scene is that it's so easy to be conventional.'
> Dench: 'And get settled . . .'.) At first she would react cautiously, there
> would be tension between her and Antony . . .

What the 1953 photographs indicate is, firstly, that Cleopatra's
court is full of attendants who constantly have to be ready for their
mistress to throw a tantrum, and secondly that Cleopatra likes to be
in control of the displays that take place in it. 'What a relief to act
Cleopatra and *cause* suffering for a change,' says Ashcroft (*Daily
Express*, 29 April 1953), known for her success in a range of victimised
female roles, including Cordelia. It seems that the reviewers who see
a cold Cleopatra here find it difficult to watch Ashcroft being selfish
and controlling. There are moments when reviewers read Dench as
successfully less than likeable – Peter Kemp in the *Independent* finds
that she 'keeps you aware of the peevish insecurity of the mistress
behind the swagger of the Queen, the crafty calculation and occa-
sional panic, the stagey luxuriatings in her own performance' (11
April 1987). However, most reviews find her an eminently empathetic
Cleopatra: 'no-one could be more real' enthuses Michael Billington
(*Guardian*, 11 April 1987), and however badly she behaves, her behaviour is always understandable, readable within realist convention. 'In
the midst of a polite and fawning court, they are excessive and parad-
ing, larger than life. She can be cruel, vulgar, perverse, emotional,
animal' explains Tirzah Lowen, giving an account of a discussion had
in rehearsal of Act I, scene iii. 'It is only when away from him that she
can reveal her vulnerability and fear of aging' (Lowen, p. 13). The play
'is about two middle-aged people – carnal, deceitful, often sad – seeking love in a reality greater than themselves' concludes Billington.

The challenging, shifting otherness of Cleopatra is rendered explicable by this empathetic, naturalistic reading.

Reviews of Ashcroft's performance are remarkably contradictory. Some mark her as startlingly honest and sincere, others as calculating and controlling. It is fascinating to compare the ways in which reviewers either manage to reconcile her paleness and red wig with their preconceptions of how Cleopatra should look, praise Ashcroft's accomplishment in working against her appearance, or leave the theatre mildly disappointed at her failure to conform to their notions of exotic sensuality. In the *Western Daily Press* (30 April 1953), Ashcroft's red wig does not work against Cleopatra's exoticness, but almost becomes a metaphor for it – 'flaming red hair that one could well imagine burning like the sun above the golden sands of Egypt'. David Lewin does not even need to re-read red hair as Egyptian, but simply makes pallor stand for darkness: 'Peggy Ashcroft looks truly alarming. Her pale face and red wig – with fringe and lashing horse tail – suggest a dark, overblown harpy' (*Daily Express*, 29 April 1953). Evidently 'alarming' is not quite good enough for Lewin, however. He remarks that, to him, Ashcroft 'lacked beauty and allure' and later adds that 'her costume revealed a waistline of 25 inches (bust 36½; hips 37½)'. Though he does not indicate whether he considered these to be Cleopatra-like measurements or not, their inclusion seems at some level to attempt to contain the alarmingly dark harpy of the red wig. Judi Dench, on the other hand, though similarly reviewed in terms of mild surprise that this English actress should manage Cleopatra so well, is more comfortably recognisable as a middle-aged woman who is attractive, passionate and funny, but past her prime and aware of it. Both she and Antony are, as Billington's review suggests, flawed but humanly so, consistently readable as psychological subjects.

What is fascinating about the contradictory critical readings of Peggy Ashcroft's performance is how well they sit with the impossibility of motivating Cleopatra in conventional realist terms. It is as difficult for the critics as it is for any audience member to decide when Cleopatra is sincere, when performing. Even Ashcroft's less enthusiastic reviewers are happy when Cleopatra is mourning Antony or dying, as here she seems most absorbed in a recognisably conventional tragic moment, less bewilderingly unreadable. At her death, the *Nottingham Guardian* reviewer, whilst he approves of the way she 'uses words like whips to subjugate [Antony] and enflame the senses', almost seems to breathe a sign of relief as Ashcroft once more becomes the 'golden girl' of the British theatre, serenely capable of exuding tragic truisms: 'dead on her throne [she] has the look that the dying often have, the smile of recognition that love and death may be the same thing in the end, the answer to life's riddle' (30 April 1953). Despite these attempts at tragic and moral recuperation, what I read in the accounts and images of Ashcroft's performance is her own interpretation of Cleopatra as 'a vile woman, a wonderfully vile woman' (*Daily Express*, 29 April 1923). Her shifts from aristocratic hauteur to manipulative sensuality are at once repellent and engaging, refusing the madonna/whore, English/foreign binaries that require frigidity from pale women with red hair, and sweet sincerity from Peggy Ashcroft.

The critical word count for both Michael Redgrave's and Anthony Hopkins's Antony is smaller. The press in both 1953 and 1987 contain articles featuring Ashcroft and Dench; the Antonies are given no such attention. Positive overall, the reviews generally agree that Redgrave and Hopkins each offer a 'noble ruin'. There is some debate as to whether Redgrave is convincingly in love, and a number of complaints about a mannered and guttural delivery. Several reviews comment on both actors' physical suitability for the part and it seems that this is one reason for paying them less attention – there is no disparity between expectation and realisation here, between physique and role, or English virtue and foreign amorality.

Cuts in the 1953 performance text remind us that squeamishness about elements of this play did not die with Dryden or the Victorians. A more decorously heroic, noble Antony is produced by these cuts than is to be found in F1. Most of his strategic reasons for leaving Cleopatra's court at the end of Act I, scene ii, after Fulvia's death has been announced, are cut (I.ii.172–87), giving a strong impression of guilt and regret, that in the full text is mixed with soldierly pragmatism. Caesar's account of Antony's urine-drinking exploits (I.iv.57–72) are cut, as are Antony's argument that he 'could not help' Fulvia's attacks on Caesar (II.ii.73–7), and that 'poisoned hours had bound [him] up from [his] own knowledge' when he was with Cleopatra (II.ii.97–8). Thus Antony is seen neither as too distastefully masculine in his behaviour, nor to be giving effeminate excuses for failing to be so. The political nature of Antony's marriage to Octavia is downplayed by cutting Menas and Enobarbus's blunt commentary at II.vi.116–20 and 124–7. The whole of Act III, scene i, is cut, ridding the play of an ignoble contrast between the Generals' feasting in the galley scene and the realities of war. Antony's vicious suggestion that Caesar should kill his slave in payment for Antony's whipping of Thydias (III.xiii 51–6) is cut, as is a great deal of the fatalistic farewell to the servants of Act IV, scene ii. Whilst Cleopatra's 'infinite variety' is staged almost in its entirety, contradictions in Antony that might render him unsympathetic disappear. Anthony Hopkins's role, on the other hand, is barely cut at all. The later production appears happier to embrace the contradictions in his character. It is interesting that there is little critical commentary on his less sympathetic actions, however. The production appears to have made the difficult and inexplicable palatable without resorting to cutting.

A more self-controlled, brutal Caesar than in F1 also emerges from the 1953 cuts. Marcus Goring's Caesar is repeatedly remarked upon as cold, calculating, tight-lipped and austere by reviewers, 'every inch and gesture the patrician, every thought the man who knew what he wanted and how he was going to get it', as clear a contrast to Redgrave's emotive warmth as that between the Egypt/Rome colours on the cyclorama. He appears to find Cleopatra's kneeling to him in Act V, scene ii either curious or faintly distasteful according to the photograph published in the *Birmingham Post*, in which he stands aloof to look down at her, placing one hand protectively on his breast. Though one reviewer describes the farewell between Caesar and Octavia as 'touching' (*Birmingham Mail*, 29 April 1953) it would surely have been more touching still if his actual goodbye had been retained: III.ii.36–41 are cut. Enobarbus's and Menas's banter about Caesar and Antony weeping, which soften Caesar by suggesting there are tears in his eyes at this parting (III.ii.51–60), also go, as does the more comforting of his long speeches to Octavia when she returns to him as go-between (III.vi.82–93). In Hall's sparsely cut production, reviewers remark upon the fastidiousness of Caesar, his reluctance to make physical contact with figures other than Octavia. Again, the production invites a psychological reading, this time, via Tim Pigott-Smith's performance, of a neurotic frigidity.

The 1953 production, then, is recognisably of the second half of the twentieth century in the simplicity of its design and fluidity of action – but also recognisably only just post-war in its cuts and its use of blacked-up attendants for a white Cleopatra. Its citation as theatre history and British golden age has done something to erase the contradictions it contained at its initial reception, which, although enthusiastic, was unsure what to make of Ashcroft. By 1987, *Antony and Cleopatra* has been allowed to spill beyond the proscenium arch; audiences are surrounded by armies as they run down the aisles onto the stage. The production's concentration on Antony and Cleopatra as two difficult middle-aged characters playing out their problems against a backdrop of mythic grandeur clearly both made psychological sense to audiences and satisfied a desire for well-spoken, beautifully designed Shakespeare. Despite minimal cuts, it too managed to paper over the awkward cracks in this productively difficult play.

The Globe, 1999

Director: Giles Block.
Antony: Paul Shelley; *Cleopatra*: Mark Rylance.

This 'original practices' production at the reconstruction of Shakespeare's Globe theatre attracted most critical attention for its swift shifts between comedy and tragedy, and for its all-male casting. These two elements are closely related. Despite Rylance's disavowal of the significance of his maleness – 'I'm playing a role which happens to be a female one, not impersonating a woman' – all-male casting was in part responsible for the comic strain in the production. This was not because Rylance deliberately drew attention to his gender, but because the necessity to 'act female' as well as to 'act Cleopatra' foregrounded the work of 'personation' done by the queen in the play. As Michael Billington puts it, 'the chief gain of having a man play the role is not any spurious "authenticity" but the way it highlights the character's histrionic excess' (*Guardian*, 2 August 1999). Whatever this Cleopatra is pretending to be, there is clearly a part of her enjoying the pretence enormously – whether groaning in frustration at Antony's absence or flicking lengths of fabric at him in fury at his dry-eyed reaction to Octavia's death. The fact that Mark Rylance is so evidently not-Cleopatra in a way that naturalistic casting must partially erase, gives an added exuberance to the work of pretence and offers the audience not only Cleopatra's lines and actions to laugh at, but Rylance's decisions as to how to perform them.

Performance by a man also seems to allow this Cleopatra a comedic enjoyment of sex and sexuality. She relishes the image of Antony on his horse with a groan of pleasure that is repeated when master and horse are next mentioned in the scene. Her line on her third entrance – 'Where is he?' (I.iii.1) – is lent a ludicrous urgency by the fact that she is wearing handcuffs. Antony has clearly left her wearing them before abandoning their bondage game when a 'Roman thought' took him. Even Toby Cockerell's Octavia gets a laugh on a lustful glance she casts at Antony on her exit, with Caesar, from Act II, scene iii. Rylance cannot draw to him the heterosexual male gaze that reviewers have bestowed (often critically) on actresses in this role; he does not try to act the mystery and allure expected of a modern Cleopatra, or when he does, it is clearly only acting. This carnivalesque sexuality should, perhaps, be disturbing or distasteful, like laughter at a misogynist drag-act. However, Rylance is not only a powerful presentational performer who knows how to ride the laughs, how to shift from address to an individual audience groundling to a broad gaze across the galleries. His performance also has an empathetic, Stanislavskian quality. This Cleopatra undermines her own 'becomings' and attention is drawn to femininity as a construct rather than a natural state of being. As Susannah Clapp remarks,

> it is interesting to see every gesture and wheedle of Cleopatra's as an act of will, and often as something unnatural. . . . [She] is a woman who plays at being a girl; there is always something gruesome about her ploys and caprices. . . . She is most human when she ceases trying to be ultra-feminine. (*Observer*, 8 August 1999)

However, whilst the combination of male gender and day-lit stage never invites one to believe he *is* Cleopatra, the clarity of intention in this performance still produces the illusion that there is someone to believe in, someone Rylance is sticking up for as well as standing in for.

I do not want to focus entirely on the 'authentic' decision to use an all-male cast here, or the very probably inauthentic decision to have a middle-aged man play Cleopatra, but rather on the kinds of meanings produced by theatrical space at the Globe. The comic tone of this production is created not only by Mark Rylance in his auburn curls. The demands that this particular stage space and its audience make on performance mean that the play's focus has to shift from psychology of 'character', as in much recent production, to theatrical space and status. The ways in which figures on this stage play for control and command of space and audience, the ways in which they take centre stage and are undermined there, produce laughter. I have not included the Globe's production in this section because it has been generally hailed as one in a line of great productions (though Billington does mention that 'not since Judi Dench' had he 'seen anyone bring out so clearly Cleopatra's humour or capacity for self-dramatisation'). The tone of many reviews is one of mild surprise at having enjoyed it so much. Far from being acclaimed as Good Theatre, the Globe has drawn repeated criticism from very different sources: for being a tourist attraction and a museum, and therefore not a home for sensitive, Stanislavskian, character-based acting or creative design; for being a tourist attraction and a museum, and therefore not a site for the radical or transgressive. There are some problematic performances in most productions there. Subtlety at the Globe is produced by the relationship between verse rhythm and movement across the large stage, and by shifts of focus from fiction to audience, from groundling to seated playgoer. Performers attempting to externalise the rhythms of naturalistic acting lose light and shade; there has been quite a lot of shouting on this stage. However, *Antony and Cleopatra* worked here in ways that point to how space produces meaning in Shakespeare.

In Act I, scene i, Antony tells Cleopatra that he cares nothing for Rome and its messengers: 'Let Rome in Tiber melt . . . | . . . here is my space' (I.i.35, 36). The actor can choose to make his 'space' Egypt, with an open-armed gesture; or, as in a number of recent productions, he might hone in with relish on Cleopatra and make his space the one between her legs. At the Globe, the large, open, day-lit stage space gives the line another meaning. From the moment Cleopatra enters this space, a battle to control it begins, which Antony is in constant danger of losing to the queen. Mark Rylance's Cleopatra flits around the Globe stage, changing direction, throwing herself onto cushions, leaving only to reappear with a swiftness facilitated by the production's fast and fluid staging. Antony is left standing helplessly, still in the 'authority position', as Pauline Kiernan named the centre of the platform stage at the Globe (Kiernan, *Shakespeare's Theory of Drama*, pp. 63–4): it has been seriously undermined as a place from which to command authority. When he announces that 'this is my space', then, he crosses the stage to where Cleopatra has momentarily come to rest and encloses her in his arms from behind, stopping her from running about in that space. Rylance's continual movement and unexpected changes of pace make Cleopatra a restless character; she flits around the stage excitedly, enthusiastically, then distractedly, unable to be at peace. Movement also allows her to possess the space. As soon as Antony has the measure of the space between them, Cleopatra changes it.

For Cleopatra's attendants, the stage space is less of a place for performance, more of a place of work. One does not have the impression of the whole court willingly indulging in Alexandrian revelry, so much as of a group of affectionate but occasionally weary servants having to tend to their mistress's needs, placing cushions for her whereever she chooses to alight. Act I, scene v, opens with a purposeful walk across the stage from one door in the *frons* to another by Charmian, Iras and company. They are interrupted and obliged to stay by Cleopatra, who changes direction to indulge her dreams of Antony. There is one moment where Charmian takes the stage, at I.v.70; she mimics Cleopatra's tone and movements, praising Caesar as her mistress now praises Antony. Though this is an amusing moment, it is interesting that Charmian does not quite manage her mistress's fluidity of movement or command of the stage. Instead she chooses to act 'end on', moving from side to side near the 'front' of the platform stage in exaggerated pantomime. It is made instantly clear that Cleopatra is the real performer here.

Antony, too, weakens his command of the space by coming to the 'front' of the platform to deliver his few soliloquies. This is a productive weakness, to the extent that it renders him vulnerable in the presence of the audience: he admits to us, for example, that he has desired Octavia's death, and appears rather desperately to be pleading for our support in 'breaking off' from the 'enchanting queen' (I.ii.125). It would have been effective to see him centre stage alone momentarily, however – to be given a fleeting sense of the power he might once have commanded. Pompey and Caesar use the 'authority position' to good effect, after all. Pompey looks out at the audience, self-satisfied, on the line 'The people love me and the sea is mine' (II.i.9). Caesar stands there deliberately ignoring 'the common body' he so despises (I.v.44) as he receives his messengers. Antony does appear more aware of the relationship between status and space during the triumvirate parley, where having asked Caesar to sit in his own home, he remains standing himself. When alone or on stage with Cleopatra, though, his battle for command of the space is repeatedly lost.

The visible audience, surrounding the stage at the Globe, draw continual attention to the public nature of the actions and interactions in the play. Cleopatra, of course, is clearly playing to both fictional and actual audiences. Negotiations between the male characters – the Octavia marriage deal for example – are signified by a shift towards the edge of the stage, as if we too must witness the contract to make it legitimate. Consciousness of being watched draws attention to the performativity of words in this play – by which I mean their power to perform actions upon characters who speak them or to whom they refer. Caesar and Antony speak and shake hands, and we know Octavia will become Antony's wife. Cleopatra bids farewell to Antony at I.iii.100 with a ceremoniously low curtsey, and she becomes a gracious but submissive lady before her knight. The broad gestures, appropriate to the size of the space, combine with the painstakingly researched costumes to draw attention to the production of social status by the donning and doffing of hats. All this social *gest*, to use Brecht's term, adds another layer of complexity to Cleopatra's continually shifting performances. There is a sense in this theatre of every figure performing a public role that only becomes meaningful when witnessed.

By the end of the production, however, self-conscious performance – particularly Cleopatra's performance of femininity – is consciously dismantled and replaced with something that makes a significant statement about performance and agency. Having reached the apotheosis of comic performance as she drags the messenger about by the hair in Act II, scene v, Rylance's Cleopatra follows Plutarch in the devastated, self-abused state in which she is portrayed in the monument (see p. 109). The auburn curls have gone, and Cleopatra is presented in a filthy shift, with a patchily shorn head – a broken human body to match Antony's heavy, bleeding one, which must be hauled to the Globe's gallery. We are presented with the simple but ghastly materiality of human death. The humour of the production does not end with the discarding of Cleopatra's femininity and royal wardrobe, however: 'Antony's bungled suicide comes across like a scene in the worst sort of minor opera', asserts Katherine Duncan-Jones (*Times Literary Supplement*, 6 August 1999), 'except that we are entirely free to laugh at it, which is a relief. His precarious abseiling up to the Monument is also, as it should be, a nail-biting stunt – "here's sport indeed!" '. In Cleopatra's exchange with the clown, too, the play's shifts in tone are emphasised as 'the clown who brings the poisoned asp . . . forgets court procedure and parks himself familiarly on the throne where the suicidal monarch is just about to turn herself into an icon' (*Independent*, 31 July 1999). Cleopatra kneels to kiss the clown's feet before he exits, as if to acknowledge that she is about to relinquish life and centre stage once she has re-made herself for the last time, covering her bleeding scalp and shift with her 'best attires'. Far from making a simple statement about the superficiality of performance and the authenticity of the raw human form, this Cleopatra demonstrates that agency is attained through *theatrical* power.

This is not a flawless production. There are unproductively awkward moments, ensemble scenes – in Pompey's gallery, for example – where the cast cannot seem to fill the space with the energy, sound and physicality required. It is a raw and exciting one, though, that offers the story and self-conscious theatricality of the play rather than a virtuoso display of psychological subtlety.

Royal Exchange, Manchester, 2005

Director: Braham Murray.
Antony: Tom Mannion; *Cleopatra*: Josette Bushell-Mingo.
Design: Johanna Bryant.

Manchester's Royal Exchange is a theatre-in-the-round built inside a Victorian cotton exchange; it is a futuristic pod of a space surrounded by ornate pillars and mouldings, bars, box office and shops. One has, on entering, a sense of theatre for sale as one of a range of tasteful commodities. For Braham Murray's production of *Antony and Cleopatra*, a more exotic bazaar is evoked by the North African music and incense emerging from the theatre space as the audience congregate around the bars and shops. Johanna Bryant's set is simple. Two moveable platforms represent Egypt and Rome; Egypt is, predictably, a warm, golden world, Rome a cold, grey and silver one. Cleopatra's platform bears a large golden scarab that can be lit golden red from the inside. The pre-set is very much of the queen's world; we are invited into it by the music and the incense and the play opens as the blue mosquito net covering the Egyptian platform is lifted to reveal Cleopatra astride Antony. On entering the building we view the 'marvellous piece[s] of work' in the craft shop's glass cabinets, then come into the theatre to see Cleopatra revealed from beneath her netting. This evocation of beauty commodified is apt for the play and is a theme that pervades a production very much centred on Josette Bushell-Mingo's Cleopatra.

Costumes take up the theme of Egyptian warmth/Roman chill, with Cleopatra and her women dressed in corset-like bodices and robes of black and gold. Josette Bushell-Mingo's dress is more casual than that of her servants. The servants are the site for a display of conspicuous consumption, whilst Cleopatra can afford to lounge around in trousers and a loose gold jacket. Romans show their wealth more subtly in pale greys and blues; for battle, armour breastplates are added to military suits. Rather oddly, the suit trousers are tucked into biker boots.

Iras and Octavia are doubled, and the transformation wrought upon Gugu Mbatha-Raw by the judicious use of wig and costume is remarkable: a mixed-race actress is black in Cleopatra's court and white in Caesar's household, objectified differently in each. As one of Cleopatra's heavily decorated waiting women she is part of the exotic display that fronts the Egyptian court; as Caesar's sister, in a dress of blue and white and a blonde wig, her beauty becomes the prized, pale modesty that can be used to seal a faltering battle partnership. Though the Egyptian costumes make the women obvious objects of sexual and economic display, Octavia is clearly powerless in ways that members of Cleopatra's self-consciously playful court are not. Octavia's dress covers her from neck to toe, and as she arrives, like 'a market maid to Rome', the contrast is clear. Octavia's modesty makes her marketable; Cleopatra markets herself.

The self-conscious playfulness and display integral to Cleopatra and her world are in full evidence in Bushell-Mingo's performance. I will undoubtedly appear critical, by comparison, of Tom Mannion's Antony, which seemed ill defined beside Bushell-Mingo's detailed and consciously theatrical performance. The problems Mannion has with the role are productive ones in the context of a wider commentary on the play, however. Bushell-Mingo's success begs some questions as to how Shakespeare's Antony, and the actor playing him, should work with the determined upstaging written into Cleopatra's role. Lyn Gardner's *Guardian* review (2 March 2005) describes this challenge as 'the harder task of making Antony seem tragic rather than just a wimp' and argues that Mannion 'does it well, suggesting a decent man floored by a fatal lack of self-knowledge and control'. I am going to argue that the self-knowledge that Antony shares with the audience in the play is underplayed in this production, making Mannion's task harder still.

From the opening of the play, Bushell-Mingo commands the stage space with her self-conscious histrionics and emotional displays; her court is an extension of herself. She plays the shifts from anger to humour, play-fainting to genuine distress with a swiftness and contrast that provoke incredulous laughter in the audience. It is simply impossible to know when Cleopatra is playing and when sincere. There is a theatricality to even her most heart-rending tears, her wildest tempers, and we are never offered the privileged access of soliloquy that might reveal what is true, what is play. Bushell-Mingo's Cleopatra appears genuinely angry with Antony's hesitations over hearing the messengers in Act I, scene i, profoundly hurt and bewildered by his marriage at the end of Act II, scene v, but even at these points one is aware that Cleopatra knows she is being watched. At the emotional high points of this performance, her anger and distress are like that of a spoiled but intelligent child who, whilst being genuinely overwrought with fury or grief, knows her tears will bring the family running. When the action is not centred on her, this Cleopatra simply does not know how to behave and runs away. In a dramatic representation of Actium, Cleopatra is lowered from the rigging on a platform, from which she watches Antony and his oarsmen; she becomes distressed and tearful as the battle appears not to be going his way – but distress and tears have no effect on battles; her retreat is signified by the raising once more of the platform. Bushell-Mingo does not offer an emotionally naïve Cleopatra, however. In her own world, centred as it is on the machinations of love rather than of battle, she appears supremely knowing.

The indeterminacy of Mannion's Antony is of a different and artistically more problematic nature. He is well able to break down in furious despair at Cleopatra's betrayals, but where Bushell-Mingo is as much Cleopatra when at play as when in torment, Mannion seems to lack energy when not in emotional crisis. 'Antony is definitely the weaker vessel in this battle of the sexes' writes Natalie Anglesey (manchesteronline.co.uk, 1 March 2005), and she describes him as 'a faded shadow of the glory that was Rome [who] descends rather hurriedly into madness after defeat'. Lynne Walker is more positive in the *Independent* (9 March 2005), praising Mannion as 'most sympathetically played', but it is notable that the 'many dimensions' she finds in his characterisation, all denote Antony in crisis: 'the hero weakened by wild infatuation, the warrior driven demented by ghostly visions and the man devastated by the magnitude of his miscalculations'. It is difficult to believe in the sexual attraction between this pair, despite the embraces in which they are revealed at the opening; it is as though Antony plays his sexual relationship with Cleopatra as Caesar and Philo see it – it saps rather than energises him. Moments when the audience might be seduced by the idea of a love that eschews responsibility and statecraft are not played up. It is almost as if Mannion is deliberately foregrounding the challenge posed by the gap between myth and reality in this play as an impossible one for the actor. Antony's attempts at self-dramatisation appear defeated from the outset. The performance lacks moments of over-blown self-belief, and the contrasting moments of self-knowledge offered in soliloquy. In the Globe production, Antony continually loses the battle with Cleopatra for centre stage – at the Manchester Royal Exchange he does not even appear to enter it.

This effect of predetermined defeat emerges partially from the fact that performers in this production never address the audience. The production establishes a fourth – or rather curved – wall between performer and auditorium. In the case of Cleopatra, this matters little. She is so clearly and continually performing to an on-stage audience, and Bushell-Mingo is so well aware of the humour and histrionics in her role, that she acquires the theatrical energy generated by the moment of direct address by other routes. She does not need to look at us, so perfectly aware is she that we are looking at her. The lack of attention to the palpable presence of the audience in the theatre-in-the-round certainly serves the men poorly, however. Terence Wilson plays Enobarbus, for example, with a successful mix of bluff pragmatism and sincere admiration of Antony and Cleopatra, but our emotional involvement in the moment of his death is limited by the production's failure to take advantage of his role as commentator throughout the play. The closeness of the visible audience to the player in this space and the intimacy of the theatre-in-the-round cry out for the urgency and vulnerability of direct address, and its absence loses Mannion's Antony an important source of theatrical energy. In soliloquy, he uses the convention of the vague and sweeping gaze around the auditorium. 'I must from this enchanting queen break off' (I.ii.125) is not spoken as if to elicit our support for a change of direction, but comes across as if Antony is simply rather tired of Egyptian revelling.

Steven Robertson's very youthful Caesar speaks of and addresses

Antony as if there were more of a muscular energy to admire in the General, at least in his battle-hungry, horse-stale-drinking past. Lynne Walker's interest in the fact that 'just as Antony abandons duty for love, so . . . Caesar abandons love (his sister, Octavia) for duty' seems misplaced. For this Caesar, love and duty appear as one. He is boyishly enthusiastic about what Antony once was, sorely disappointed at his compatriot's descent into seediness, and delighted at the match between the General and his sister. The lingering kiss between brother and sister at Octavia's parting seems an irrelevant psychological detail, when Caesar's true love seems to be for an idealised father figure in Antony. The alliance with Octavia is just the kind the Antony of his *Boy's Own* dreams should make – it rescues the General from the clutches of a love match and returns him to the arms of pragmatic duty. Caesar is angry and disillusioned at his hero's betrayal of his sister, but in Cleopatra's presence cannot help but betray an excitement at the possibility of recuperating and reclaiming some of Antony's notoriety by having the queen in his power. Even when denied his own Cydnus moment by Cleopatra's suicide, Robertson plays Caesar's speculations as to the method of the queen's death with a boyish excitement: the story may not have turned out as he had planned, but at least he is at the centre of something grimly glorious which will earn him a place in history next to his comrade.

Rome is not a place of spectacle but of action, and in this production there are two moments that highlight the respectively awkward and disastrous results of inaction for this masculine world. The first is the staging of the triumvirs' counsel of Act II, scene ii, when after the momentary inaction of 'Sit . . . Sit sir . . . Nay then' (ll. 31–4), Antony and Caesar do so – at opposite ends of the playing space on small plinths at ninety degrees to the larger Roman and Egyptian stages. The effect of leaving such a large gap between two actors attempting conversation is an odd one; for a moment it is as if no one thought to make the plinths portable so a more natural proximity could be achieved. Ultimately though, it highlights the impossibility of anything but violent action as the basis of the relationship between the men. The attempt at parley leaves an awkwardly empty stage space, pregnant with the possibility of future battle between the two. Only bringing a woman into the space as a bartering tool can momentarily close the gap.

The second hiatus of inaction is one created by a dramatisation of Cleopatra's retreat at Actium. The male ensemble assemble a boat from the shiny mirrored shields to be used in later battle scenes. Antony drums a rowing rhythm at the head of the boat, then stops and pauses as Cleopatra is lowered on her platform. The men stop rowing; a few of them get to their feet; all look at Antony for leadership, which fails to materialise. A moment of hesitant inaction is all that is needed before the whole boat is disassembled in a rush, and Antony's fleet is routed in the mind's eye. Compare this with the triumphant recovery of Antony's battle fortunes in Act IV. This fills the stage with a chaos of men, all leaping in the air and bringing down their swords into the rubber-stone flooring, then pulling them out and leaping again, demonstrating the furious effort needed to stab body after fallen body. Where the climactic moment of the Actium scene is one of hiatus then chaos, here the chaos of battle shifts to something more choreographed, as the soldiers make a circle round Antony, stabbing their swords into the ground around him in a frenzied rhythm. Antony wins when he is at the centre of the action, fails when Egypt tempts him to inaction.

The production's simple set works well at Cleopatra's death, offering what early bare-stage productions might have done by way of monumental display: Cleopatra in her best attires is her own monument. Seated upright on her golden scarab, at peace and with her eyes closed, she has frozen herself in time just as she would wish to be remembered. In death, Bushell-Mingo's Cleopatra achieves a more dignified form of public display than the emotional posturing of her life. Given the strength of this moment, and the touching simplicity of the deaths of Charmian and Iras before it, the production might have permitted the clown his comic moment. Joseph Mawle plays a faintly fey and sinister fool; he is clearly meant to presage death and might therefore have been better replaced by Everal A. Walsh, the Soothsayer.

Cleopatra, Charmian, Iras, the eunuch Mardian and the Soothsayer are played by black British actors in this production, and a modern British audience may not necessarily have associated their appearance with the North African flavour of the opening. The Soothsayer, particularly, is dressed as a witch doctor of sub-Saharan archetype. He seems alien to both Rome and Egypt in the solemnity of his traditional spirituality. A black actress as Cleopatra, however, works on a range of levels in a modern production. The fact that I have considered whether these actresses are of the right ethnicity to play Egyptians may provoke the reader to wonder why I have not questioned the fact that Robertson's blond Caesar would be hard pushed to pass for Italian. Roman-ness in Western culture is not marked on the body in the way that Egyptian-ness is, despite the literal marks on the body that bring about a Roman death. A black Cleopatra encourages a (largely white) British audience to confront their own racism and ask how far white British society still regards the black population as exotic, or threatening, other. The combination of Bushell-Mingo's race and her ease with the stage space leads to the inevitable association of Rome with an uptight white establishment, threatened by both celebration and miscegenation. Bushell-Mingo's race signals as nothing else could do that Antony is taking a step outside his own culture and knowledge, a fact paradoxically underpinned by the fact that the marriage arranged by his fellow countrymen is to Octavia, played by an actress who 'passes' as white.

Like Antony, it is in the East where Braham Murray's production finds its pleasure – and indeed its most engaging pains and tensions too. One could argue that this is inevitable – that love, jealousy and domestic friendship between women are inevitably more accessible to a modern audience than Roman battle plans. It is a pity in this respect that the galley scene is cut, with the whole of Pompey's role, as this might have given the audience a window into the human foibles of the masculine world of the play to balance our intimacy with its female side. I leave the Manchester Royal Exchange, however, feeling that the space invites even the most formal of Romans to address us directly, and that the pace of Murray's radical cut of the play is slowed by the lack of urgency in terms of performer/audience relationship. A remarkable Cleopatra wins the battle for theatrical status outright and it would have been exciting to see her obliged to fight harder for her victory.

5 The Play on Screen

Antony and Cleopatra has not been particularly successful on film or television. The film image most likely to come to mind in association with the story is of Cecil B. de Mille's film, or Elizabeth Taylor in Joseph Mankiewicz's Hollywood epic *Cleopatra*, an extravaganza that inspired *Carry On Cleo*, one of the series of low-budget, British seaside-postcard-style comedies. None of these have much relationship to Shakespeare. The fact that more film directors have not considered making a large-cast epic of the Shakespeare play itself suggests, perhaps, that the kinds of public intimacies the play offers do not lend themselves to a film vocabulary. As Richard David has suggested, 'to switch to and fro between one and another of the elements in a crowded scene, destroys a characteristic Shakespearean effect, which derives from the simultaneous contemplation of opposing forces and their interactions' (David, in Bulman and Coursen, *Shakespeare on Television*, pp. 139–40). His critique is of the limitations of television Shakespeare, but a similar point could be made about film. Though film clearly facilitates crowd scenes in a way the small screen does not, it deals with tensions and confrontations in the presence of a large groups by cutting from figure to figure, so that the sense of a battle for theatrical status and space is lost.

The only film of Shakespeare's play is Charlton Heston's 1973 production, which has been shown on American television but never released in the cinema. Of four television productions, the most recent was directed by Lawrence Carra in 2001. This is the first since Jonathan Miller directed the BBC Shakespeare series version in 1981. The most successful TV version is Jon Scoffield's film of Trevor Nunn's 1972 Royal Shakespeare Company (RSC) production; the performances are developed and Scoffield makes good use of simple film techniques to create a range of locations and a sense of space. The three-part BBC *Antony and Cleopatra*, produced in 1963 as the third of their Roman plays series, *The Spread of the Eagle*, is no longer available in video form.

Lawrence Carra directs Lynn Redgrave and Timothy Dalton, 2001

The play is filmed on a wooden stage with an entrance that recalls the tiring house of a Jacobean theatre in a façade upstage, with a platform above it. Curving staircases extend from either end of the platform and frame the central entrance. The performers look cramped and slightly too large for the stage. Caesar's train, complete with red standards and Roman costumes that recall those in Mankiewicz's epic, is unintentionally comic, as the soldiers trot down what little space the staircases offer them, to the sound of trumpet flourishes.

Lynn Redgrave is a cheerful, somewhat innocent-seeming Cleopatra in her first scenes, an interpretation that might have developed productively had she had more room to make more of a swift and skittish range of movements. She drives Antony to fury with her teasing, then switches to softness and sincerity when she is in danger of driving him from the stage. Her child-like behaviour here allows her to grow up convincingly as she mourns Antony. In the monument she becomes calmer and more self-ironising, despite having nothing to battle with when it comes to hauling Antony in with her (he is pulled rather limply up one step). She is mother to her women in the monument, where earlier she plays their spoiled child.

Timothy Dalton also played Antony in Toby Roberton's production for Theatre Clewyd in 1986, with Lynn's sister Vanessa as Cleopatra. Then, he was accused by reviewers of being 'far too young and vigorous and alert' (*The Times*, 1 June 1986). Fifteen years later, when he is genuinely middle-aged, his longish hair and striped North African garb in the first scenes smack, appropriately enough, of a faintly pathetic attempt at grooviness. Dalton's performance works best when he is in dialogue with the triumvirate and Pompey; here he makes a convincingly relaxed Antony. His demise is the more painful because he has convinced himself that he is in control, at least of the male world of battle strategy. With Cleopatra he is deliberately more unpredictable – mortified and furious, for example, at her teasing in Act I, scene iii. This is valid, and suggests that only she can make him lose his temper. In the parley of Act II, scene ii, Antony is rendered the more relaxed and in control by Caesar's shouting; more shouting obliterates the irony in Caesar's reaction to Antony's letter in Act IV, scene i. Pompey, too, seems put to more than 'some impatience' (II.vi.41–2) by the smiling, reasonable Antony. Irony is once again lost in furious ranting. Menas offers a refreshingly dry delivery, and his plausible friendliness towards Enobarbus reminds the viewer that, though Caesar describes the Roman world of war as all honest, manly rigour, within these soldierly encounters lies the potential for deceit and cruelty.

The declamatory tone of this production finally works in Cleopatra's favour. It is a relief to reach the stillness of the monument and to watch her attain her rather elegant, tuneful death – she leaves the world on a long, high-pitched cry. From the odd video box inlay (which, despite the English leads, promises that there will be no confusing English accents to baffle the viewer) through to the pastiche Elizabethan music that accompanies the final titles, however, this is a surprisingly amateurish and outmoded production, especially given some of the well-known faces on the screen.

BBC Shakespeare: Jonathan Miller directs Jane Lapotaire and Colin Blakely, 1981

The critic should not comment unfavourably on Jane Lapotaire's prickly, unsensual Cleopatra in Jonathan Miller's production for the BBC Shakespeare series without considering his avowed intention to work against Hollywood stereotypes of steamy sensuality. Miller claims that 'Cleopatra's sexuality and prowess were myth, not grounded in history' (Bulman, in Bulman and Courzen, p. 55). In the play, however, this seems to be a myth in which Cleopatra and many who come into contact with her believe, and in Miller's production it is difficult to imagine how or why. Kisses are all bestowed on the hand. The delicate silks and pearl earrings worn by the queen and her attendants are based on Italian Baroque art – Miller cites Veronese's 'The Family of Darius at the Feet of Alexander' as a source, and favourable reviews of the production emphasise the resultant rich, pictorial qualities of the production, rather than the rich sensuality of the central figures.

One of Lapotaire's more striking moments is her death scene, in which her quiet delivery and gaze off camera in close-up produce a moving effect of genuine belief that she is going to meet Antony. Oddly, there are two full kisses on the mouth leading up to this – one by way of a goodbye to Charmian, plus the one that seems to kill Iras – which makes the lack of sexual contact with Antony seem all the more deliberate on Miller's part. Lapotaire has a lovely self-ironising relationship with the aged clown who brings the asp – an asp that gets more of a sensual stroking than Antony ever does. Her earlier prissiness in contrast with this scene, then, produces a narrative in which a spoiled upper-class woman who imagines she is in love discovers real intimacy and sensuality in suicide.

There is little of the play's exposure of personal tensions in public in this production, as attendants and soldiers are often squeezed out of the frame. H. R. Courzen is furious at the lack of the 'Herculean Roman' in Antony here (Courzen, in Bulman and Courzen, p. 273), but Colin Blakely is a soldierly, down-to-earth Antony who is convincingly losing control from the outset; one can imagine his men's affection for him and his loyalty to his forces in battle, which makes his retreat at Actium the more shocking. His hearty farewell to the servants in Act IV, scene ii is a moving moment and his strangled cry of 'Not dead? Not dead?' is daringly agonised.

Ian Charleson's is a new take on the cold, conventional Caesar of many productions. He does indeed seem a stickler for convention, but this allows him to appear at ease, rather than repressed, when convention is being followed, and plausibly irritable and awkward when it is not. He is at his most sympathetic saying goodbye to Octavia, wanting to believe in the marriage and its propriety, but worried at leaving her with Antony nevertheless. Then on Octavia's return, he seems too humiliated before his men by the *impropriety of* her mode of travel to show her any affection. In Act IV, scene vi his treatment of Enobarbus is vicious: he speaks the plan to put deserters in the front line against Antony straight to the soldier's face; the gesture suggests a contempt for deserters who do not follow a code of loyalty. This is an interpretation that productively limits Caesar's capacity for humanity, by suggesting not that he is a repressed psychological oddity, but that his subjectivity is produced by gender and class convention. It is appropriate, then, that on hearing of Antony's death in Act V, scene i, he moves away from the camera, leaving Maecenas and Agrippa to discuss his indecorous tears in near close-up.

As several critics have commented, the use of depth in this production is one of the more effective aspects of its camera work. Figures in the foreground commenting on those in the background, for example Cleopatra and Enobarbus looking on at Antony's good-bye to his servants, go some way to undoing the flattening effect of the small screen. Though these shots cannot create the effect of a court or an army witnessing the protagonists' exchanges, an effective tension is produced as those being watched are evidently unaware of it. As Richard David notes, when figures in the foreground fade at these points, their 'critical presence' is 'not entirely forgotten' (David, in Bulman and Courzen, pp. 140–1). It could perhaps have been used to offer another perspective on Enobarbus's death, movingly performed but with no soldiers as witnesses.

Address to camera is used only by Enobarbus, as he considers Antony's demise and his own possible desertion of the General. This is reasonably effective in the moment; Emrys James offers a dry, bluff but sympathetic performance common to many in the role, and the moment of conspiracy with him is engaging.

Miller seems to have felt the lack of what the theatre suggests in terms of imagined off-stage spaces. He cuts scenes in which characters look out over battlegrounds and is thus in danger of giving the impression no battles happen at all. This may be why Plutarch's account of Actium appears on screen at the beginning of the second half of the production, before Act III, scene xi. This use of another – written – text is in danger of signalling the inadequacy of the form of television for the play. It might have worked interestingly if it had

occurred more often alongside the use of other texts and images –
Courzen suggests the use of an early map of relevant parts of the
world (in Bulman and Courzen, p. 271). Ultimately, however, this is
a production that decides that it cannot be theatre, but in trying to
be painting will not quite let itself relinquish the consistency of TV
realism.

Trevor Nunn/Jon Scoffield direct Janet Suzman and Richard Johnson, 1974

In adapting Trevor Nunn's RSC production for television, Jon
Scoffield makes no attempt to hide the fact that he is filming in a
studio. Outdoor shots, particularly those of figures appearing from a
distance, and shots from above, create imagined and symbolic rather
than representative spaces. On his return from Actium, Antony is
seen from above, walking alone across a sandy-coloured studio: we
imagine him alone in his shame and in a desert landscape. Caesar and
his followers stride purposefully across a cold, white expanse: we
imagine a walk to the senate. Soft-focus is used to blur Cleopatra's
world, as if the early Alexandrian revels, and the queen's approach to
Antony after his victory in Act IV, scene viii, take place in a dream.
Where props and set are used to create a more realist setting – filmy
curtains and big cushions for Cleopatra's court, for example – these
always spill outside the shot, creating a boundless fictional space for
the action. Crowds are not avoided – they are filmed occasionally
from above, and sometimes close-up and as if from within, so that
the viewer has a sense of what it might be like to be at a galley party
of sweaty Roman soldiers, or in the middle of a battle amidst clash-
ing swords and dying groans. Sound sets many of the scenes –
lapping waters or the far-off barking of dogs again ask the listener to
imagine a landscape, rather than attempting to re-create one.

The blurred, dream-like quality of the film-making makes something more than cliché of Suzman and her Egyptian court, even
though they are mostly played by white actors with a lot of tawny
pan stick. After the self-consciously Egyptian title sequence, the
camera pans across a line of soldiers in black and white, as Philo

complains of Antony's degeneracy, then cuts to the gauzy, golden glow of an Egyptian scene in which Cleopatra rides Antony through her drunken court. Whose Egyptian fantasy is this – Philo's prurient one, Cleopatra's contrivance, our own Western one?

Of the screen performances analysed here, this is the most self-consciously performing Cleopatra. Having teased Richard Johnson's Antony to bewildered distraction in front of the court in Act I, scene i, her every line and gesture to him in the first Acts of the play is tinged with irony. Moments where other Cleopatras cease to perform and offer sincerity, for example during Act I, scene iii, are almost parodied here, and where the text offers clear opportunities for teasing performance – the formal farewell of I.iii, for example – Janet Suzman always takes them. Even where she admits her love for Antony to her attendants there is a playful sense of self-ridicule in her performance. This is a queen used to being in control but who also knows that power is fragile and that she must always be watching and waiting for moments to secure it. Her equivocation in battle is only logical – where she cannot be sure of winning it is safer to retreat. Her tactics are unscrupulous, and whereas in I.i and I.iii they are appealing in their energetic theatricality, her insistence on the sea battle in Act III, scene vii, is unpleasantly manipulative. Antony seems inclined to listen to the soldier who implores him not to 'fight by sea'; Cleopatra sees that Antony is paying him heed and stalks huffily from the tents where the discussion is taking place. Antony looks helpless and follows.

Johnson's Antony steadily loses control through the course of the production, and this clearly disconcerts, even revolts Cleopatra. This is underlined, not unsubtly, by references to drunkenness, and not only at obvious points such as Act I, scene i, or the galley feast. As Antony angrily explains to Octavia his differences with her brother in Act III, scene iv, she is dishevelled as if aroused from sleep. Antony takes a drink in this 'bedroom' scene, which she appears to notice, worriedly. Cleopatra is quietly thoughtful throughout the Thidias sequence, and though there is no sense in which she appears to be anything but happy and proud at Antony's recovery after his wild behaviour, she will not join in the revels of the last 'gaudy night', which extends into the farewell to the servants. Rueful at the way he has let down his compatriots from the outset but utterly besotted and bewildered by Cleopatra, Antony is always ready to drown his sorrows.

My description of these performances might lead to the conclusion that Suzman's is a cold performance, Johnson's a pathetic one. They are, however, richly drawn and engaging figures, partly in comparison with the extreme chilliness of Corin Redgrave's Caesar. Distant, sneering and particularly unpleasant to Lepidus, whom he never misses an opportunity to undermine, Octavius makes Antony and Cleopatra's fantasy world seem rich and inviting, even as it crumbles. Patrick Stewart's Enobarbus, too, with his real relish of Cleopatra and her barge performance, reminds us that Cleopatra is capable of taking anyone – with the exception of Caesar – with her on a voyage of sensual discovery. Pompey's remarks about the queen of Egypt (II.i.21–7) are not included, as this version follows the tradition of cutting him entirely. The galley scene is retained in part, simply as a soldier's feast and an example of the ridiculous figure Antony might become if he follows Lepidus's example. It is also an opportunity for Caesar to show his utter contempt for those who allow themselves to lose control in any way, as Lepidus is carried unconscious from the scene.

This is a self-consciously filmed production rather than an attempt to translate the play via the conventions of television realism. As such it cleverly foregrounds notions of perspective, as we wonder whose version of events we are watching. Suzman give a look to camera in an early sequence that suggests that ultimately it is hers, and her dignified self-control in death certainly supports this impression.

Charlton Heston directs: Charlton Heston as Antony; Hildegarde Neil as Cleopatra, 1972

The opening credits of Heston's film, in which he also plays Antony, appear over a calm sea, with a boat sailing across it – a small, primitive one, very much of an ancient world in which travelling is precarious and slow. The sequence introduces the sea as the backdrop and central metaphor for the film. Much of its grandiose Egyptian scenery and unrelenting orchestral music will seem dated to viewers today. It contains some impassioned ranting from Heston that recalls, rather unfortunately, his performance in *Planet of the Apes*. It is drastically cut and the sequence of scenes is reordered. However, it is interesting in its use of extras representing indigenous populations, and its recurring water imagery.

The boat sails into harbour and up to a rough jetty. A Roman soldier – a messenger in Act I, scene i – disembarks and rides through the narrow streets of a small Egyptian town, evidently caring little for its occupants, whose market wares and families he scatters as he goes. This is the first of the film's foregroundings of the Egypt Cleopatra might 'unpeople' if she wished. Actors playing indigenous Egyptians appear as the market townspeople, as galley slaves rowing Antony's ship at Actium, as a somewhat ill-equipped army. The triumvirate parley of Act II, scene ii takes place at Caesar's small personal Roman game' ring, in which two more hapless plebeians – a gladiator and a slave – fight for their lives throughout the scene for his entertainment. The fight is a violent subtext to the irritable parley: we cut from the vicious, enforced game to the faces of Caesar and Antony. Eventually the slave pinions the gladiator with a fork through the arm, and Caesar lets the former live with a casual thumbs-up.

Though Cleopatra's aristocratic status is clear in the distinction made between Alexandrian town and court life, her status within the drama is much reduced by this film. Hildegarde Neil's is a white Cleopatra, accompanied by Jane Lapotaire's very English Charmian. Even the common touch suggested by Antony's comment on her desire to 'wander through the streets and note / The quality of people (I.i.55–6) is cut. In fact, for the purposes of this film, her racial and cultural otherness from Rome does not need emphasis, as the important way in which she is 'other' to Antony is in being female, his nemesis but also his natural destiny.

If Cleopatra becomes less of a character and more of a love object in the film, Octavia's role is reduced still further. Act II, scene iii is transposed to follow Act III, scene iii, so we do not see Antony with his new wife until we have received the partial account of her from

Cleopatra's terrified messenger. In this version, Antony makes tentative sexual overtures to Octavia, who modestly rejects them with her 'Goodnight sir' (II.iii.8). A forlorn and frustrated Antony hears Cleopatra's sensual tones as voice-over, then stumbles upon Enobarbus giving the 'barge' speech, transposed from Act II, scene ii, to a group of attendants. Forced to recognise that i'th' East his pleasure lies, Antony makes off for Egypt to the sound of the swelling orchestra. On Cleopatra's magnificent front steps, the greeting which, in the play, comes after Antony's battle victory of Act IV, scene viii, is used for the reuniting of the lovers. The 'world's great snare' that Antony has come from 'uncaught' (IV.viii.18) has become dispassionate Roman duty, represented by a frigid Octavia.

At the battle of Actium, which Heston films in full, Cleopatra is clearly playing at sea wars, wearing a pretty silver helmet fashioned as if from fish-scales. The ships heave into battle, and at first Antony's forces are shown to be doing well; there is an impressive scene in which the huge hull of his ship rams a Roman one and his men board it for a fight that is shot from within – a mess of weapons, blood and falling bodies. Cleopatra, the cosseted princess in her battle fancy-dress, is unsurprisingly unsettled by finding herself in the thick of the action, so that there is no ambiguity about her retreat. She flies because she is afraid. Antony must follow his destiny: he sees Cleopatra's ship turn, and is given Agrippa's line of Act IV, scene vii, 'Retire, we have engaged ourselves too far,' which evidently they have not. The man who must beat the retreat for the slaves below deck looks hesitant and horrified. The face of a smiling Caesar and a shamed Antony fade up over burning ships and drowning men.

The sea is a recurring image in this film. It is used to cross-fade one scene into another and as a reminder of the elements that play a part in the harsh life of a soldier in the ancient world. Unsurprisingly, it also represents the feminine. Alexas has to swim to Cleopatra's luxurious floating raft to deliver his message of Act I, scene v. After Actium, Antony crawls from water onto sand, then, during the encounter with Cleopatra of Act III, scene xi, attempts to burn his hand in a candle flame. It is as if at this point he does not know how to punish himself enough, how to get dry enough. When Eros disarms him he sinks his master's armour in the calm water through which the two have just rowed, Antony telling Eros that his 'visible shape' can no longer hold (IV.xiv.14). The manly conflict of love and duty has been resolved – the water has claimed his soldierly side and Antony is now all for love.

Nevertheless, Heston is featured throughout the last scenes of the film as a lone and desperate figure, riding and staggering towards his end in the archetypal filmic quest for masculine identity. The awkward suicide attempt is underplayed, as there is no request from Antony for passing soldiers to finish the job or bear him to Cleopatra. Instead he stumbles all the way to the monument himself and dies in her arms on the much-altered line 'No-one but Antony did conquer Antony.' Neil is at her strongest in her dealings with Caesar in the monument – cool, ironic and dignified – then dies with a quiet delight, stretching out to Antony's body in her last moment, then falling back where Caesar finds her, on a bed next to her lover. It is a pity that in so much of the film she is not permitted to provide more of a challenge, rather than a cipher, to the notions of masculine destiny and identity on which Heston's film centres. Antony, it seems, must die because elements of his masculine subjectivity – the social that would bind him to Rome and the sexual that would bind him to Cleopatra – are in conflict. His manful stagger to Cleopatra's monument and invented dying line resolves that conflict too easily.

6 Critical Assessments

As they die for each other, we forgive them for having lived for
each other.

(Augustus William Schlegel, c.1809)

Now we feel the pressure of our 'mating' references throughout,
the constant stress on 'melting', 'dissolving', 'mingling', till
'strength' of eternity and 'force' of time are inextricably 'entangled'
... and 'death', misnamed phantom, but the simplification, the
freeing and loosing of life's 'intrinsicate knot'.

(G. Wilson Knight, 1931)

after giving a faithful picture of the soldier broken down by
debauchery, and the typical wanton in whose arms such men
perish, Shakespeare finally strains all his huge command of
rhetoric and stage pathos to give a theatrical sublimity to the
wretched end of the business, and to persuade foolish spectators
that the world was well lost by the twain.

(George Bernard Shaw, 1934)

as [Antony and Cleopatra] transgress the power structure which
constitutes them, both their political and personal identities ...
disintegrate.

(Jonathan Dollimore, 1984)

Here are extracts from four critical accounts of the ending of *Antony
and Cleopatra*. It seems logical and tidy to place them in chronological
order. I do not want to suggest that critical opinion of the play has
somehow *progressed* from the romantic views of Schlegel in the early
nineteenth century to the materialist ones of Dollimore in 1984, via

Wilson Knight's close reading and Shaw's arch cynicism in the thirties. Though critical ideas and vocabulary such as Dolllimore's are distinctively late twentieth-century, arguments not unlike Schlegel's are still echoed in work published as late as 1992, as Sara Munson Deats has pointed out in her survey of *Antony and Cleopatra* in criticism (Deats, p. 2). However, placing criticism in its historical moment enables the scholar better to explore how it can be used and developed, engaged with and argued against. In examining critical writing on *Antony and Cleopatra*, it is worth considering not only what the critics have found in play, but what they wanted to find and what it was possible for them to find at the time their opinions were formed.

What the reader may notice immediately about the quotations above is that the first and third take a moral stance on the play and its characters, which the second and fourth do not appear to do. Schlegel assumes a unity of response in his use of 'we': he puts 'us' in the position of forgiving moral judges. Shaw would presumably regard Schlegel as one of his 'foolish spectators' here, and judges the lovers much more harshly. Knight, though his transcendentalist tone does suggest an underlying approval of Antony and Cleopatra, appears more concerned with how redemption is achieved through poetry than morality. Dollimore does not make moral judgements in anything like the same way; even from this fragment it is clear that he does not read character as Schlegel or Shaw do. Schlegel finds classical prototypes for Antony and Cleopatra in Hercules and Omphale (see pp. 99–100); he is best known for his translations of Shakespeare into German and for his arguments for the structural unity of Shakespeare's plays, and his view of Cleopatra is influenced by the gender archetypes of his time. However, like the novelistic criticism that was to follow, his commentary seems to suggest a mixed, contradictory and psychologically plausible character too: Cleopatra is 'made up of royal pride, female vanity, luxury, inconstancy, and true attachment' (Schlegel, in Brown, *Antony and Cleopatra*, p. 28). Shaw appears to regard the lovers even more clearly as moral archetypes, hence his irritation at what he perceives to be Shakespeare's attempt to redeem the irredeemable. They are still to be judged, however, as one might judge a real public figure whom one perceives to have acted wrongly of his or her own free will. What Dollimore is interested in, on the other hand, is not psychological motivation or morality, but dramatic figures – and indeed pieces of writing – as constructs of their social, historical and political position. In 'Antony and Cleopatra: Virtus under Erasure', he argues that in the early seventeenth century there has been a shift from the 'power of the titular aristocracy' with its ideology of virtus or individual valour, to the less visible power of the state (Dollimore, *Radical Tragedy*, p. 204). He analyses Antony's desires and disintegration, then, as they reflect the disintegration of old power structures and residual ideologies. Here his project is radically different from Knight's, too, where Knight reads the play for its intrinsic poetic power, a power that to an extent is framed as existing outside its historical moment.

A reader familiar with any of the kinds of criticism mentioned here and below will have noticed that a varying amount of notice is taken of the theatre and theatrical production in academic work on Shakespeare. Whether critics be aiming for romantic proof of tragic greatness, novelistic analysis of character, a close reading of language and imagery or politicised historicism, not all of them are as conscious of the theatrical rhetoric of the plays as Shaw is when he warns those 'foolish spectators' of the ways in which Shakespeare can work on the mind and the senses. Theatrically oriented criticism is not the preserve of the late twentieth century, as readers of Harley Granville-Barker's still influential *Prefaces to Shakespeare* will know. However, a strong wave of 'stage-centred' criticism, interested in the way an understanding of Shakespeare's theatrical conditions of production might inform readings of the plays, emerged in the 1970s and 1980s. The principles of this work, together with more recent performance criticism concerned with the meanings made in production today, provide a useful counterpoint to character-based, poetic and cultural materialist criticism alike.

As is clear from the performance history of *Antony and Cleopatra*, the eighteenth century did not regard it highly. Audiences favoured Dryden's re-writing of the play, *All for Love*, with its stricter adherence to the classical unities of time, place and action; Shakespeare's perceived lack in this respect is much criticised by commentators of the time. 'The scene is sometimes in Rome, sometimes in Egypt, sometimes at Sea and sometimes at Land' complains Charles Gildon, 'and seldom a line allow'd for a passage to so great a Distance' (Gildon in Steppat, *The Critical Reception*, p. 15). As early as the mid-eighteenth century, however, there were commentators who saw the limitations of imposing classical decorum on Shakespeare. Dryden's play was 'most correctly poetical with the unities' comments an anonymous critic, but *Antony and Cleopatra*, 'tho' one of the most incorrect and careless of Shakespeare's plays . . . [is] most pathetically Natural without 'em' (anon. in Steppat, ibid., pp. 15–16). Indeed, Dr Johnson admits that it is the 'frequent changes of the scene' that give the play its 'power of delighting'. He is clearly engaged by what are later recognized as the strengths of Elizabethan and Jacobean dramaturgy: 'The continual hurry of action, the variety of incidents, and the quick succession of one personage to another, call the mind forward without intermission from the first Act to the last' (Johnson, in Brown, *Antony and Cleopatra*, p. 26). The moral tone of most eighteenth-century commentary is condemnatory of the lovers. Typical is Francis Gentleman, for whom 'a double moral may be inferred' from the play, 'namely that indolence and dissipation may undo the greatest of men; and that beauty, under the direction of vanity, will not only ruin the possessor but the admirer also' (Gentleman, in Bains, *Annotated Bibliography*, p. 261).

Nineteenth-century critics tended to regard the play as less impressive than *Hamlet*, *Macbeth*, *Othello* and *King Lear* but were delighted by its scope and the energy and grandeur of its poetry – the '*feliciter audax*' or 'happy valiancy' to which Coleridge famously referred (Coleridge, in *Coleridge's Shakespeare Criticism*, p. 86). The Romantics saw successful unity of design where the Enlightenment had found indecorous untidiness. 'It presents a fine picture of Roman pride and Eastern magnificence: and in the struggle of the two, the empire of the world seems suspended,' writes Hazlitt (Hazlitt, in Brown, *Antony and Cleopatra*, pp. 29–30), at the beginning of a long and still thriving critical tradition that sees the play as structured around the binary opposites of Rome and Egypt. Coleridge finds profound moral analysis of Cleopatra's character in the play and seems willing, despite an essentially negative moral judgement of Cleopatra, to embrace her contradictions:

the sense of criminality in her passion is lessened by our insight into its depth and energy, at the very moment that we cannot but perceive that the passion itself springs out of the habitual craving of a licentious nature, and that it is supported by voluntary and sought-for associations. (Coleridge, *Coleridge's Shakespeare Criticism*, p. 86)

Moral debate around character dominates nineteenth-century criticism of the play, with more romantically inclined critics such as Schlegel arguing that the central figures redeem themselves through love – a romantic transcendentalism that has lasted well beyond the Romantic period: Charles Wells still argues in 1992 that in *Antony and Cleopatra* '[w]e are confronted with the startling thought that love of two individuals can outweigh piled centuries of disembodied state' (Wells, *The Wide Arch*, p. 165). The nineteenth century nevertheless had its cynics, with the likes of Hartley Coleridge finally condemning the lovers: 'perhaps both Antony and Cleopatra are too heroic to be pitied for weakness and too viciously foolish to be admired for heroism' (H. Coleridge, in Deats, *New Critical Essays*, p. 183).

A. C. Bradley developed the character-based approach to Shakespeare into the twentieth century – indeed he is regarded as the father of character criticism, which has tended to analyse figures in sixteenth- and seventeenth-century plays as if they had emerged from nineteenth-century novels. He assumes that 'we' are readers rather than audience members – 'we close the book in a triumph which is more than a reconciliation' (Bradley, *Oxford Lecturers on Poetry*, p. 304). He expects clarity of character and motivation in his drama and finds it necessary to excuse or criticise when this is not forthcoming; he considers that Shakespeare was little interested in Caesar, for example (pp. 288–90). Bradley was also concerned, as were many critics of the first half of the twentieth century, with the genre of *Antony and Cleopatra*. For him, *Antony and Cleopatra* does not quite reach the heights of tragedy – 'it is not painful' (p. 282), it does not contain anything 'overtly either terrible or piteous' (p. 287). The engaging and triumphant nature of the lovers' deaths ultimately makes the play generically flawed: 'we are saddened by the very fact that the catastrophe saddens us so little; it pains us that we should feel so much triumph and pleasure' (p. 304).

Later in the twentieth century, the question of whether *Antony and Cleopatra* is truly a tragedy becomes less of a concern for critics of Shakespeare; many have come to regard the playwright as quite justifiably adapting his sources according to the needs of his theatre, rather than in line with strict generic decorum. Janet Adelman's influential *The Common Liar* argues that 'the insistence upon scope, upon the infinite variety of the world, militates against the tragic experience. . . . The protagonists find themselves to be of primal significance in the universe, but we must see them from other, less comfortable perspectives' (Adelman, p. 49). For her, the play offers a 'tragic experience embedded in a comic structure' (p. 52), as it plays with the audience's engagement with and critical distance from the action. Marilyn French neatly dismisses the need to find strict Aristotelean tragic structure in *Antony and Cleopatra* – 'A fall, a flaw, a recognition' – as reductive (French, *Shakespeare's Division of Experience*, p. 254). David Bevington, in his introduction to the play, still feels the need to defend the play in terms of its tragic credentials, though he considers an Aristotelian model unhelpful. He draws upon Walter Oakeshott's and Dorothea Krook's readings of Shakespeare's use of Plutarch to argue that 'Antony and Cleopatra establishes its own sense of genre – one in which . . . the concept of tragedy is enriched and complicated by the heroic' (Bevington, p. 32, drawing upon Krook, *Elements of Tragedy*, pp. 184–229). Thus though the deaths of Antony and Cleopatra are triumphant, 'that triumphant ending does not gainsay the suffering and the tragic experience that have led to it' (Bevington, p. 32, drawing upon Oakeshott, 'Shakespeare and Plutarch', pp. 111–25).

The first half of the twentieth century sees a variety of challenges to the character-based approach of A. C. Bradley. Harley Granville Barker's *Prefaces to Shakespeare* return to Shakespeare's open stage for a defence of this play's geographical scope, and for his analysis of Cleopatra. The *Prefaces* analyse the plays in the light of the theatres and companies for which they were written. Instead of judging Cleopatra as an example of female waywardness and treachery, redeemed or not through death, Granville-Barker reminds the reader that she was originally played by a boy, and that 'wit, coquetry, perception, subtlety, imagination, inconsequence' (Granville-Barker,

p. 84) are the qualities such a boy might have portrayed as opposed to a steamy sensuality. Granville-Barker's theatrical reading has influenced later theatre practitioners and stage-centred critics, and its intelligent lack of misogyny is refreshing: he points to what a Jacobean production company would have made of Cleopatra, rather than regarding her as some universal epitome of the female, as we will see feminist commentators accusing male critics of doing, below.

If one was to place Granville-Barker at one end of a continuum between theatrical and literary criticism, G. Wilson Knight might occupy a place at the literary end. His work on the play also goes beyond Bradley's preoccupation with character study, concentrating instead on the symbols and figurative language of the play. Knight's redemption of Antony and Cleopatra occurs poetically, as Shakespeare's imagery shifts from 'the material and sensuous, through the grand and magnificent, to the more purely spiritual' (Knight, *The Imperial Theme*, pp. 204–5). For Derek Traversi, language reconciles contradictions in the play, as

> The gap between what is clearly, from one point of view, a sordid infatuation, and the triumphant feeling which undoubtedly, though never exclusively, prevails in the final scenes, is bridged by a wonderful modification of connected imagery.   (Traversi, *The Roman Plays*, p. 219)

For the student of the theatre, poetic close reading of Shakespeare may have its limitations. A deft and elegantly written analysis such as Frank Kermode's in this vein, for example, assiduously points out the many ways in which Shakespeare uses the words 'world' and 'becoming' in *Antony and Cleopatra* (Kermode, *Shakespeare's Language*, pp. 217–230), but one is occasionally left wondering how these repetitions make meaning in the theatre. More useful for a consideration of the play in production are more theatrically aware close readings. The work of critics such as John Russell Brown considers the play's imagery and its 'broken verse lines, metrical irregularities, short phrases and unusual word order' in terms of its challenges for actor and audience (Brown, *The Tragedies*, 2001, p. 322). Maurice Charney's essay 'The Imagery of *Antony and Cleopatra*' demonstrates how

Shakespeare's imagery works theatrically, for example in his analysis of '[t]he basic application of sword and armor imagery' (Charney, p. 151). In his detailed reading of the play's scenic structure, Emrys Jones points to the effect that its 'uniquely expressive poetic style' might have on its audiences (Jones, *Scenic Forum*, p. 237).

As Yashdip S. Bains suggests, the twentieth century sees an increasing willingness amongst critics to accept that *Antony and Cleopatra* is a morally ambiguous play, and perhaps deliberately so. As early as 1938, Derek Traversi argued that two seemingly contradictory readings of the play – as 'a tragedy of lyrical inspiration, justifying love by presenting it as triumphant over death' and 'a remorseless exposure of human frailties' – are both essential and integrated themes (*The Roman Tragedies*, p. 208). Julian Markels starkly states that 'Shakespeare makes us amoral', as Antony refuses to choose between 'public and private values' (Markels, *The Pillar of the World*, p. 191). As we have seen in Jonathan Dollimore's work, it is the late twentieth century's politically inflected studies of theatre as material, gendered and colonialist culture that finally turn away from moral judgement and debate as to the essential meanings encoded in the plays.

Dollimore is one of a number of self-styled cultural materialists, predominantly British academics, who are often associated with the American New Historicist critical movement which emerged during the 1980s. Both groups were influenced by philosophical analyses of ideology and power written by Althusser and Foucault, who argued that whereas each individual experiences him/herself as the origin of his or her actions, each is in fact the instrument and effect of societal power structures. Since the 1980s and 1990s, the ideas of New Historicism and cultural materialism have been debated, developed and disputed. I draw attention to these movements once again, though, as they mark a break in Shakespeare criticism away from an underlying obligation to find what is supposedly universally and morally recognisable in the plays, towards the analysis of what is historically and politically distinctive about them. Politically oriented historicist criticism of the late twentieth and twenty-first century, moreover – be it based in Marxist thought, as is Dollimore's cultural materialism, or in feminist or postcolonial or queer theory – aims to examine its own historical moment too. These critics reject the idea of a timeless, universal meaning to be discovered in Shakespeare, for an analysis of how meaning is made in production and reception now and in Shakespeare's time.

These politicised approaches are often described as being underpinned by 'theory' – an unhelpfully vague term which suggests that what came before was somehow *not* based on a theory of how dramatic literature or the social world works. A number of works in this very broad field may frustrate the student of theatre. Some critics appear to read plays as cultural and historical documents rather than as artistic and theatrical ones, failing to take into account the ways in which a play is structured to create, say, pleasure or suspense, rather than merely to reflect or interrogate the social world. Dollimore argues that *Antony and Cleopatra* and *Coriolanus* 'effect a sceptical interrogation of martial ideology' (p. 204), but does not make clear how this scepticism might have worked, say, upon an audience waiting in eager anticipation for the famously empathetic Burbage to speak Antony's lines. On the other hand, much writing inflected with cultural theory of this postmodern turn does specifically deal with theatre production and reception, both in Shakespeare's time and now, whilst other works open up issues of representation that can usefully be related to theatre production.

Given the play's preoccupation with the exoticism of Cleopatra and Egypt, postcolonial criticism's challenge to white Western assumptions about race and representation is particularly pertinent to an analysis of *Antony and Cleopatra*. Edward Said's seminal account, in *Orientalism*, of how Western representation fixes the East as a different and dangerous 'other' to the West, underpins and has been explicitly cited in these readings. Postcolonial criticism figures Cleopatra as black, pointing to the fact that although the historical queen was Greek, Shakespeare's character is conjured by Rome as 'non-Roman, nonwoman, black woman, witch, slut, bitch, Egyptian, African' (Little, *Shakespeare Jungle Fever*, p. 145). In the essay whence comes this list, Arthur Little sees Enobarbus's reading of Cleopatra as that of the ethnographer and the pornographer, exoticising and objectifying the foreign and the female. Ania Loomba shows how 'dominant notions about female identity, gender relations and imperial power are unsettled through the disorderly non-European woman' (Loomba, *Gender, Race, Renaissance Drama*, p. 125). For both Loomba and Little, Cleopatra and Egypt challenge and disturb Rome even in the moment of Caesar's final triumph, as Cleopatra 'not only cheats Caesar but denies final and authoritative textual closure' (ibid., p. 130). Carol Chillington Rutter's *Enter the Body* is primarily concerned with the representation of gender on stage, but her chapter on *Antony and Cleopatra* challenges the ways in which twentieth-century productions of the play have erased historical evidence of her theatrical blackness.

A number of late twentieth-century critics have sought to redefine or challenge the notion that Egypt and Rome represent cultural and gender opposites in *Antony and Cleopatra*. This binary has been central to much criticism of the play in the nineteenth and twentieth centuries. Dollimore's essay, on the other hand, points to ways in which Antony and Cleopatra, Rome and Egypt are similar rather than different in their need to display and define themselves through power (pp. 215–17). Feminist critics have returned to the Egypt/female, Rome/male binary, and, like Loomba and Little, have posited the Egyptian, feminine principle as a threat or alternative to the male order. Though patriarchal Rome may define itself as the centre of order and civilization, Marilyn French asks 'how civilised is this civilising principle?' and answers, 'Roman values – order and degree, power-in-the-world, structure and possession – do not create harmonious order. . . . They create contention and rivalry, one order superceding another and thin, pleasureless, stiff existence' (p. 265). Cleopatra's Egypt, on the other hand, is 'unified, wholly itself, it is powerful and not on the moral defensive. . . . It's great threat lies in its great appeal and its lack of respect for "masculine" qualities. . . . It is thus anti-civilisation; yet it is the principle of life' (p. 256).

In an earlier and influential feminist reading, Linda Fitz examines the 'sexist attitudes' of nineteenth- and twentieth-century critics who have found Cleopatra seductive, unfathomable, morally repellent or a combination of all three. Fitz questions the notion that Cleopatra's motives are impossible to explain and relates it to the misogynistic idea that all women are somehow unfathomable. 'Shakespeare has taken pains to let Cleopatra explain her contrary behaviour and give reasons for it (I.iii)', Fitz argues. 'In short, Cleopatra needs to be demythologized. What she stands to lose here in fascination she stands to gain in humanity' (in Drakakis's *Antony and Cleopatra*, p. 202). Fitz's points are sharply argued and her examples from male critics, from Dowden in 1875 to her own age, are startling. However, this early piece of feminist Shakespeare criticism posits Cleopatra as a figure in a realist drama and blames male critics for failing to recognise her motives as psychologically plausible. In demanding that we 'demythologize' Cleopatra, Fitz ignores the complex ways in which Cleopatra re-enacts, colludes with and unsettles her own mythology.

Linda Charnes, who lists an exhaustive list of postmodern theorists as her influences for *Notorious Identity,* is acutely aware of the ways in which 'notorious' mytho-historical figures in Shakespeare appear both to have agency and to be trapped within their already-known narratives. For Charnes, Cleopatra's power lies in her ability to present herself as unpenetrable spectacle, as opposed to the passive object of a gaze such as Caesar's:

> By presenting surface only, an experience of pleasure that does not permit penetration . . . spectacle also denies voyeurism, which depends on controlling not only the image of the object but its meanings as well. Cleopatra as self-staged spectacle denies the voyeur – he can narrate the spectacle, but not determine with any confidence its 'character'.   (p. 133)

Thus for Charnes, Cleopatra renders herself unreadable, rather than having a misogynistic unreadability imposed by sexist critics.

Disappointingly little academic work has been done on the meanings produced by speculative early stagings of *Antony and Cleopatra*. A short extract from Alan Dessen's *Rescripting Shakespeare* demonstrates the potential of this approach. Dessen notes how the F1 stage directions have the sentries who are witness to the mysterious music of Act IV, scene iii, 'place themselves in every corner of the stage'. The Romans thus take clear control of the stage space, only to have that control undermined by the strange sounds emerging from beneath it. Dessen draws parallels between these bewildered Romans, the soldiers watching the willed suicide of Enobarbus, then Caesar and his men as they discover Cleopatra's death. He suggests that Roman witnesses should be similarly placed in the three scenes, 'to set up a clear, even italicised parallel between . . . moments . . . which depict both a "Roman" frame and something that cannot be contained and explained within it' (p. 164).

This kind of attention to stage space and spectacle could usefully be linked to some of the feminist and postcolonial Shakespeare criticism concerned with the politics of representation in *Antony and Cleopatra*. Analysis of early conditions of performance, and the ways in which staging may be encoded in the play texts, root Shakespeare's work firmly in the theatrical conditions in which it was produced. Historically aware, politicised criticism links it to wider ideological meanings – meanings brought to bear on a play like *Antony and Cleopatra* by contemporary and current audiences. Both theatrically and ideologically inflected readings, moreover, may be enriched by close reading of the play's imagery and internal structures. The Further Reading section of this *Handbook* aims to enable the reader to find the most productive combinations of critical approach for his or her own studies.

Further Reading

This list of recommended further reading includes a sample of recent editions of the play, three wider bibliographies and three substantial collections of criticism. In the selection of individual works, criticism with a theatrical slant, and more recent approaches to the play have been privileged, but earlier twentieth-century works concerned with language, structure, genre and character are also included.

Editions of the play – introductions

Bevington, David (ed.), *New Cambridge Shakespeare* (Cambridge: Cambridge University Press, 1990). Bevington's introduction includes summaries of critical approaches to the play and a substantial history of the play in performance, with photographs.

Jones, Emrys (ed.), *New Penguin Shakespeare* (London: Penguin, 2005). The introduction is Jones's from the 1977 print. It is a less cumbersome text for rehearsal than the more substantial scholarly editions; its notes are at the back of the volume.

Madelaine, Richard (ed.), *Shakespeare in Production* (Cambridge: Cambridge University Press, 1998). Notes on the text in this edition are replaced with detailed notes on decisions made in past productions. The introduction is a 138-page, detailed history of the play in production.

Neill, Michael (ed.), *The Oxford Shakespeare* (Oxford: Clarendon Press, 1994). Introduction includes detailed commentary on sources, performance and critical interpretation.

Wilders, John (ed.), *The Arden Shakespeare*, Third Series (London and New York: Routledge, 1995). A clear, scholarly introduction with a shorter, but still useful, performance history.

Wilders, John (ed.), *BBC TV Shakespeare*. This edition of the play shows cuts made in Jonathan Miller's BBC television production (see pp. 143–6) and includes stills from the production.

Bibliographies and critical histories

Bains, Yashdip B., *'Antony and Cleopatra': An Annotated Bibliography* (New York and London: Garland Publishing, 1998). Includes a history of criticism of the play and extracts from the entries in the bibliography.

Steppat, Michael, *The Critical Reception of Shakespeare's 'Antony and Cleopatra' from 1607 to 1905* (Amsterdam: Verlag B. R. Grüner, 1980). Includes a history of criticism of the play to 1905 and extracts from the entries.

Walker, Lewis, *Shakespeare and the Classical Tradition: An Annotated Bibliography, 1961–1991* (New York and London: Garland, 2002). Books, chapters and articles on *Antony and Cleopatra* are listed, with abstracts explaining the contents.

See also the collection by Sara Munson Deats, in the section 'Collections of Critical Essays' below.

Collections of critical essays

Brown, John Russell, *Antony and Cleopatra, Casebook* series (London: Macmillan, 1968). Comprises extracts from critical reception before 1900, criticism on the play in performance and examples of twentieth-century criticism. Includes extracts from A. W. Schlegel's essays in Dramatic Literature, 1809–11; S. T. Coleridge's Shakespeare criticism, 1808–19; William Hazlitt's *The Characters of Shakespeare's Plays*, 1817; A. C. Bradley's *Oxford Lectures on Poetry*, 1905; Harley Granville-Barker's *Prefaces to Shakespeare*, 1930; Maurice Charney's *Shakespeare's Roman Plays*, 1961, all cited in the Critical Assessments section here.

Coleridge, Samuel Taylor, *Coleridge's Shakespeare Criticism* (London).

Deats, Sara Munson, *New Critical Essays on 'Antony and Cleopatra'* (New York: Routledge, 2005). Includes Deats's comprehensive survey, 'Shakespeare's Anamorphic Drama: a Survey of *Antony and Cleopatra* in Criticism, on Stage, and on Screen' and an 'Interview with Giles Block, Director of the 1999 Production of *Antony and Cleopatra* at Shakespeare's Globe in London', by Georgia E. Brown.

Drakakis, John, *Shakespeare: 'Antony and Cleopatra'*, New Casebooks series (Basingstoke: Macmillan, 1994). Comprises a range of 'theoretically informed' criticism on the play from the second half of the twentieth century – challenges, the editor argues, to 'the idealist notion that literary texts were ultimately the repositories of universal truths about the human condition' (p. 20), with examples of feminist, cultural materialist and postcolonial criticism. Includes extracts from Janet Adelman, *The Common Liar*, 1973; Marilyn French, *Shakespeare's Division of Experience*, 1982; Jonathan Dollimore's *Radical Tragedy*, 1984; Ania Loomba's *Gender, Race, Renaissance Drama*, 1989, and Linda T. Fitz's essay 'Egyptian Queens and Male Reviewers: Sexist Attitudes in *Antony and Cleopatra* Criticism, 1977, all cited in the Critical Assessments section here.

Early conditions of production, theatrically oriented and performance criticism

These works are grouped together as they all demonstrate a consciousness of the play as theatre. Brown and Cartwright find directions and challenges for actors and audiences encoded in the play text. Dessen, though his book is generally about recent production, analyses Act IV, scene iii, in terms of early staging; early staging informs Granville-Barker's and W. B. Worthen's work. Hosley's articles are cited in Bevington's Cambridge University Press edition of the play and deal specifically with the balcony and the challenge of hauling Antony into the monument at the Globe. Andrew Gurr's book mentions the staging challenge of the monument and is an excellent guide to every aspect of early modern theatrical conditions; Keith Sturgess, though he does not deal with *Antony and Cleopatra*, provides the most substantial recent work on the indoor playhouses.

Stott's book is a short account of the play and its performance history. David Lindley's is a detailed analysis of music in both early and recent Shakespeare productions. Gamini Salgado's collection is of first-hand accounts of Shakespeare in performance. E. K. Chamber's 4-volume record of early modern theatres and companies is still drawn upon by scholars today, though some of his conclusions have been challenged. The other works in this section are concerned with the meanings produced by recent stagings of *Antony and Cleopatra*; Lowen's book deals specifically with Peter Hall's 1987 production. Scholarly reviews of individual productions can be found in the journal *Shakespeare Survey* and in *Shakespeare Quarterly*'s 'Shakespeare Performed' section.

Brown, John Russell, *Shakespeare: The Tragedies* (Basingstoke: Palgrave Macmillan, 2001).

Cartwright, Kent, *Shakespearean Tragedy and its Double: The Rhythms of Audience Response* (Philadelphia: Pennsylvania University Press, 1991).

Chambers, E. K., *The Elizabethan Stage* (Oxford: Oxford University Press, 1923).

Dessen, Alan C., *Rescripting Shakespeare: The Text, the Director, and Modern Productions* (London: Routledge, 2002).

Granville-Barker, Harley, *Prefaces to Shakespeare*, vol. 3: *Antony and Cleopatra*, pp. 1–66 (London: B. T. Batsford, 1930).

Gurr, Andrew, *The Shakespearean Stage, 1574–1642* (Cambridge: Cambridge University Press, 1992).

Hodgdon, Barbara, '*Antony and Cleopatra* in the Theatre', in *The Cambridge Companion to Shakespearean Tragedy*, ed. Claire McEachern (Cambridge: Cambridge University Press, 2002).

Holland, Peter, *English Shakespeares: Shakespeare on the English Stage in the 1990s* (Cambridge: Cambridge University Press, 1997).

Hosley, Richard, 'Shakespeare's Use of a Gallery over the Stage', *Shakespeare Survey*, 10 (1957), pp. 77–89.

Hosley, Richard, 'The Staging of the Monument Scenes in Antony and Cleopatra', *Library Chronicle*, 30 (1964), pp. 62–71.

Knowles, Richard, 'The Stratford Festival', in *Reading the Material Theatre* (Cambridge: Cambridge University Press, 2004), pp. 105–28.

Lamb, Margaret, '*Antony and Cleopatra*' *on the English Stage* (London: Fairleigh Dickinson University Press, 1980).

Lindley, David, *Shakespeare and Music* (London: Arden Shakespeare, 2005).

Lowen, Tirzah, *Peter Hall Directs* '*Antony and Cleopatra*' (London: Methuen, 1990).

Salgado, Gamini, *Eyewitnesses of Shakespeare: First-Hand Accounts of Performances, 1590–1890* (London: Sussex University Press, 1975).

Stott, Michael, *Antony and Cleopatra: Shakespeare, Text and Performance* series (London: Macmillan, 1983).

Sturgess, Keith, *Jacobean Private Theatre* (London: Routledge & Kegan Paul, 1987).

Worthen, W. B., 'The Weight of Antony: Staging "Character" in *Antony and Cleopatra*', *Studies in English Literature, 1500–1900*, no. 26 (1986), pp. 195–308.

Film and television

Bulman, J. C. and H. R. Courzen (eds), *Shakespeare on Television: An Anthology of Essays and Reviews* (Hanover and London: University Press of New England, 1988).

Davies, Antony and Stanley Wells (eds), *Shakespeare and the Moving Image* (Cambridge: Cambridge University Press, 1994).

Willis, Susan, *The BBC Shakespeare Plays: Making the Televised Canon* (Chapel Hill, NC: University of North Carolina Press, 1991).

New Historicist and cultural materialist criticism

Anyone unfamiliar with these movements in late twentieth-century criticism might explore the essay collections *Political Shakespeare*, ed. Jonathan Dollimore and Alan Sinfield (Manchester: Manchester University Press, 1994); *Alternative Shakespeares* (London: Routledge, 2002), and *Alternative Shakespeares*, vol. II (London: Routledge, 1996), ed. John Drakakis and Terence Hawkes respectively, and *Shakespeare and the Question of Theory*, ed. Patricia Parker and Geoffrey Hartman

(London: Routledge, 1990). Though none contain specific work on *Antony and Cleopatra*, they offer useful and inspiring approaches to the study of Shakespeare.

Cultural materialist work on the play is to be found in:

Dollimore, Jonathan, *Radical Tragedy: Religion, Ideology and Power in the Drama of Shakespeare and his Contemporaries* (London: Harvester/ Wheatsheaf, 1984).
Tennenhouse, Leonard, *Power on Display: The Politics of Shakespeare's Genres* (New York and London: Methuen, 1986).

Feminist/gender criticism

Bamber, Linda, *Comic Women, Tragic Men: A Study of Gender and Genre in Shakespeare* (Stanford, CA: Stanford University Press, 1982).
Berggren, Paula S., 'The Woman's Part: Female Sexuality as Power in Shakespeare's Plays', in *The Woman's Part: Feminist Criticism of Shakespeare*, ed. Carolyn Ruth Swift Lenz et al. (Urbana: University of Illinois Press, 1980).
Bushman, Mary Ann, 'Representing Cleopatra', in *Another Country: Feminist Perspectives on Renaissance Drama*, ed. Dorothea Kehler and Susan Baker (Metucha, NJ: Scarecrow, 1991).
Charnes, Linda, *Notorious Identity: Materialising the Subject in Shakespeare* (Cambridge, MA, and London: Harvard University Press, 1995). I have included Charnes's study here not because her book is specifically oriented towards gender studies in Shakespeare, but because, as I have argued on p. 162, her analysis of Cleopatra's notoriety usefully challenges Linda Fitz's early feminist essay.
Fitz, Linda T., 'Egyptian Queens and Male Reviewers: Sexist Attitudes in *Antony and Cleopatra* Criticism', *Shakespeare Quarterly*, vol. 28, no. 3 (Summer 1977).
French, Marilyn, *Shakespeare's Division of Experience* (New York: Summit Books, 1982).
Harris, Jonathan Gil, ' "Narcissus in thy face": Roman Desire and the Difference it Fakes', *Shakespeare Quarterly*, vol. 45, no. 4, pp. 408–25.

Khan, Coppélia, *Roman Shakespeare: Warriors, Wounds, Women* (London: Routledge, 1997).

Postcolonial criticism

Chillington Rutter, Carol, *Enter the Body: Women and Representation on Shakespeare's Stage* (London: Routledge, 2002).

Little, Arthur L., Jr, *Shakespeare Jungle Fever: National–Imperial Re-visions of Race, Rape, and Sacrifice* (Stanford, CA: Stanford University Press, 2000).

Loomba, Ania, *Gender, Race, Renaissance Drama* (Manchester: Manchester University Press, 1992).

Loomba, Ania, *Shakespeare, Race and Colonialism* (Oxford: Oxford University Press, 1989).

Said, Edward W., *Orientalism* (New York: Vintage, 1979).

West, Russell, 'Travelling Thoughts: (the Displacement of Identity)', in *Spatial Representations and the Jacobean Stage* (Basingstoke: Palgrave Macmillan, 2002), pp. 200–11.

Shakespeare, Plutarch, the classical world

Bullough, Geoffrey, *Narrative and Dramatic Sources of Shakespeare*, vol. 5: *The Roman Plays* (London: Routledge & Kegan Paul, 1964). This contains all the source material reprinted here, together with other possible sources and analogies.

Hughes-Hallett, Lucy, *Cleopatra: Histories, Dreams, Distortions* (New York: Harper & Row, 1990).

Kelso, Ruth, *Doctrine for the Lady of the Renaissance* (Urbane: University of Illinois Press, 1956).

Kiernan, Pauline, *Shakespeare's Theory of Drama* (Cambridge: Cambridge University Press, 1993). Kiernan's section on *Antony and Cleopatra* provides some detailed analysis of Shakespeare's use of Plutarch.

Martindale, Charles and Michelle, *Shakespeare and the Uses of Antiquity* (London: Routledge, 1990).

Martindale, Charles, and A. B. Taylor (eds.), *Shakespeare and the Classics* (Cambridge: Cambridge University Press, 2004).

Miles, Geoffrey, *Shakespeare and the Constant Romans* (Oxford: Clarendon Press, 1996).

Miola, Robert, *Shakespeare's Rome* (Cambridge: Cambridge University Press, 1983).

Miola, Robert, *Shakespeare and Classical Tragedy* (Oxford: Oxford University Press, 1992).

Seneca, *The Stoic Philosophy of Seneca: Essays and Letters*, trans. Moses Handam (New York: W. W. Norton, 1958).

Thomas, Vivian, *Shakespeare's Roman Worlds* (London: Routledge, 1989).

Wells, Charles, *The Wide Arch: Roman Values in Shakespeare* (New York: St Martin's Press, 1992).

Imagery, language and structure

Charney, Maurice, *Shakespeare's Roman Plays: The Function of Imagery in the Drama* (Cambridge, MA: Harvard University Press, 1961).

Clemen, W. H., *The Development of Shakespeare's Imagery* (London: Methuen, 1951).

Dunbar, Georgia, 'The Verse Rhythms of Antony and Cleopatra', *Style*, no. 5 (1971), pp. 231–45.

Jones, Emrys, *Scenic Form in Shakespeare* (Oxford: Clarendon Press, 1971).

Kermode, Frank, *Shakespeare's Language* (London: Allen Lane, 2000).

Knight, G. Wilson, *The Imperial Theme* (New York: Methuen, 1951).

Mack, Maynard, 'The Stillness and the Dance: *Antony and Cleopatra*', in *Everybody's Shakespeare: Reflections Mainly on the Tragedies* (Lincoln, NE, and London: University of Nebraska Press, 1992).

Traversi, Derek, *The Roman Plays* (London: Hollis and Carter, 1963).

Genre

Adelman, Janet, *The Common Liar: An Essay on 'Antony and Cleopatra'* (New Haven, CT: Yale University Press, 1973).

Bamber, Linda, *Comic Women, Tragic Men: A Study of Gender and Genre in Shakespeare* (Stanford, CA: Stanford University Press).

Barroll, J. Leeds, *Shakespearean Tragedy: Genre, Tradition and Chance in 'Antony and Cleopatra'* (Washington, DC: Folger Books, 1984).

Bevington, David, *Introduction to Antony and Cleopatra*, New Cambridge Shakespeare (Cambridge: Cambridge University Press, 1990).

Bradley, A. C., *Oxford Lecturers on Poetry* (London: Macmillan, 1959).

Krook, Dorothea, *Elements of Tragedy* (New Haven, CT: Yale University Press, 1969).

Markels, Julian, *The Pillar of the World: 'Antony and Cleopatra' in Shakespeare's Development* (Columbus: Ohio State University Press, 1968).

Oakeshott, Walter, 'Shakespeare and Plutarch', in John Garrett (ed.), *Talking of Shakespeare* (London: Hodder and Stoughton, 1954), pp. 111–25.

Character criticism

Barroll, J. Leeds, 'Shakespeare and the Art of Character: a Study of Antony', *Shakespeare Survey* (1969), pp. 159–235.

Barroll, J. Leeds, 'The Characterisation of Octavius', *Shakespeare Survey* (1970), pp. 231–88.

Bradley, A. C., *Oxford Lectures on Poetry* (London: Macmillan, 1959).

Hume, Robert D., 'Individuation and Development of Character through Language in *Antony and Cleopatra*', *Shakespeare Quarterly*, no. 24 (1973), pp. 281–300.

Stewart, J. I. M., *Character and Motive in Shakespeare* (London: Longmans, 1949).

Index

21114432R00111

Printed in Great Britain
by Amazon